ABHANDLUNGEN FÜR DIE KUNDE
DES MORGENLANDES

Im Auftrag der Deutschen Morgenländischen Gesellschaft
herausgegeben von Florian C. Reiter

Band 72

2010
Harrassowitz Verlag · Wiesbaden

Verbal Festivity in Arabic and other Semitic Languages

Proceedings of the Workshop at the Universitätsclub Bonn on January 16, 2009

Edited by Lutz Edzard and Stephan Guth

2010

Harrassowitz Verlag · Wiesbaden

Bibliografische Information der Deutschen Nationalbibliothek
Die Deutsche Nationalbibliothek verzeichnet diese Publikation in der Deutschen Nationalbibliografie; detaillierte bibliografische Daten sind im Internet über http://dnb.d-nb.de abrufbar.

Bibliographic information published by the Deutsche Nationalbibliothek
The Deutsche Nationalbibliothek lists this publication in the Deutsche Nationalbibliografie; detailed bibliographic data are available in the internet at http://dnb.d-nb.de.

For further information about our publishing program consult our website http://www.harrassowitz-verlag.de

Printed on permanent/durable paper.
Printing and binding: Hubert & Co., Göttingen
Printed in Germany

ISSN 0567-4980
ISBN 978-3-447-06239-8

Table of Contents

Preface

This volume is based on the contributions delivered at a joint workshop that the two co-editors had organized at the Universitätsclub Bonn on January 16, 2009. The immediate occasion of the workshop were the 65th birthday of Werner Diem, University of Cologne, and the 70th birthday of Michael G. Carter, University of Sydney, in January 2009. Stefan Wild, University of Bonn, also joined us on this day. All three scholars, to whom the two co-organizers of the workshop are deeply indebted, contributed intensively to the discussion during the proceedings and helped us to conceptualize the final character of this volume.

The common denominator of the one-day workshop was the theme "Verbal Festivity in Arabic and other Semitic Languages", as agreed upon by the two co-organizers. It appeared to be a reasonable idea to unite presentations about various aspects of formal and polite speech in the Semitic language area with a focus on Arabic. Stephan Guth opens the volume with a linguistic and cultural overview from a bird's perspective: "Politeness, Höflichkeit, *ʾadab*: A Comparative Conceptual-Cultural Perspective". Avihai Shivtiel continues along these lines with an overview entitled "Language and Mentality: Politeness, Courtesies and Gestures in Palestinian Arabic". Pierre Larcher in his contribution focuses on a morpho-syntactic analysis of "Formules et dérivés « formulatifs » en arabe". Geoffrey Khan addresses volitive verbal forms in his overview "The Expression of Deontic Modality in the North-Eastern Neo-Aramaic Dialects". Lutz Edzard deals with "Injunctive Protases and the Grammaticalisation of Elliptic Conditional Clauses in Semitic". Andreas Kaplony concludes the volume with an analysis of economic formulae in his article "The Interplay of Different Kinds of Commercial Documents at the Red Sea Port al-Quṣayr al-Qadīm (13th c CE)".

We wish to express our gratitude to our home institution, the Department of Culture Studies and Oriental Languages (IKOS), University of Oslo, for generous funding of this workshop.

Oslo, January 2010

Lutz Edzard — Stephan Guth

Politeness, Höflichkeit, *ʾadab*
A Comparative Conceptual-Cultural Perspective

Stephan Guth, IKOS, University of Oslo

I – Introduction

Many of the linguistic devices and techniques used to produce an atmosphere of "verbal festivity," the Bonn workshop's topic, have in common the goal to obey certain cultural norms or rules of conduct that most of us, I assume, would not hesitate to subsume under the heading of "politeness" (or "Höflichkeit," in German). But what would such a heading be in Arabic? In his entry on "politeness" in the *Encyclopedia of Arabic Language and Linguistics*, Avihai Shivtiel suggested that the most common rendering of "politeness" in Arabic is *ʾadab* (Shivtiel 2008, 658). This is of course correct on many occasions, but although the semantics of the two terms *do* overlap, there are also considerable differences in meaning because both are not simply vocabulary items but in fact history-loaden *concepts* and as such mirror the specificities of two different *cultures* and *civilisations*.

Samuel Huntington's diagnosis of a "clash of civilisations" is not so much talked about in the media anymore; yet, it has, I think, still not lost its suggestive potential in the minds of the public. And since it is still hovering around in public opinion, it remains to be important – perhaps even more so – to become clear about fundamental concepts both in our own *and* in Middle Eastern cultures, because these concepts are culturally so significant and because a one-to-one equation tends to be full of shortcomings that impede/obstruct mutual understanding.

How is this danger to be countered? From a European perspective, three things seem to be necessary:

1) to study the history of fundamental concepts in our own language (s) and to be aware of the details of their current use;
2) to try to understand as deeply as possible, and then explain to the public, the current meanings and historical development of corresponding concepts in Arabic;

3) to bring both together and identify areas of overlapping as well as of incongruence, so as to become eventually able to fulfill the task of an "intercultural translator."

In the present contribution I will certainly not endeavour to carry out this project for *politeness*, *Höflichkeit* and *ʾadab* in a comprehensive manner – any attempt to do so would be deemed to failure from the beginning because of the complexity of the subject matter and the limitedness of space available. What I intend to do then instead is to illustrate with some examples the way in which it *could* and, in my opinion, *should* be carried out, to point to research lacunas, and to present a project that aims at covering at least some of them.

II – *Politeness, Höflich(keit)*, etc. – Western concepts

In all the major European languages, I suppose, dictionaries or other reference facilities are available in which one can easily look up a word's etymology and/or its semantic development. Look, e.g., at *The Oxford English Dictionary* (2nd ed., 1989). The entries on "polite" and "politeness" both give 3 main meanings (1.-3.), some of them with subgroups (a., b., c.). For each semantic value, dated textual evidence is given, arranged chronologically, and for each meaning the entries state whether it is the literal or a metaphorical use and whether it is, as the case may be, "obsolete" (abbreviated "Obs.," for instance in 1.b. of "polite"), "[n]ow only in certain collocations" (2.a.), or "[t]he chief current use" (2.c.):

> **polite** (pə(ʊ)ˈlaɪt), *a.* Also 5 polyt, pollyte, 6 polyte. [ad. L *polīt-us* polished, accomplished, refined, cultivated, polite, prop. pa. pple. of *polīre* to smooth, polish. Cf. It. *polito* (Florio), F. *poli* (12th c. in Littré), etc.]
>
> † **1.** *lit.* Smoothed, polished, burnished. *Obs.*
>
> *c* **1450** *Mirour Saluacioun* 1485 The Arche withinne & without was hiled with golde polyt. *c* **1470** HENRY *Wallace* IX. 1082 Throu polyt platis with poyntis persyt thair. **1601** B. JONSON *Poetaster* III. i, I am enamour'd of this street now .. tis so polite, and terse. **1675** EVELYN *Terra* (1729) 8 Potters-Earth .. became like Sand .. exceeding polite and smooth. **1678** CUDWORTH *Intell. Syst.* I. v. 731 Polite Bodies, as Looking-Glasses. **1737** WHISTON *Josephus, Antiq.* xv. ix. §6 Edifices .. made of the politest stone.
>
> † **b.** Cleansed, furbished, trim, neat, orderly. *Obs.*
>
> **1497** BP. ALCOCK *Mons Perfect.* E j, Theyr monestery in every corner therof is all pollyte & clene. **1673** RAY *Journ. Low C., Glaris* 427 At Suitz .. the people .. keep their houses neat and cleanly, and withal very polite and in good repair. **1703** MAUNDRELL *Journ. Jerus.* (1721) 77 To preserve these Chambers of the dead polite and clean.

2. *transf.* **a.** Of the arts, or any intellectual pursuits, esp. literature: Polished, refined, elegant; correct, scholarly, exhibiting a refined taste. (Now only in certain collocations.)

1501 DOUGLAS *Pal. Hon.* II. viii, ȝone is .. the court rethoricall, Of polit termis. **1531** ELYOT *Gov.* I. v, That they speke none englisshe but that which is cleane, polite, perfectly and articulately pronounced. **1612** SELDEN *Illustr. Drayton's Poly-olb* vi. 98 That polite Poem (in whose composition Apollo seems to haue giuen personall aide). **1699** BENTLEY *Phal. Pref.* 49 All the Lovers of Polite Learning .. give me thanks. **1726** C. D'ANVERS *Craftsm.* i. (1727) 4 My natural inclination to the politer arts. **1786–7** BONNYCASTLE *Astron.* i. 12 One of the most useful branches of a polite education. **1824** L. MURRAY *Eng. Gram.* (ed. 5) I. 174 Every polite tongue has its own rules. **1891** *Speaker* 2 May 532/1 In it meta-physics have again condescended to speak the language of polite letters.

b. Of persons *(a)* in respect of some art or scholarship, *(b)* in respect of general culture: Polished, refined, civilized, cultivated, cultured, well-bred, modish.

1629 WADSWORTH *Pilgr.* viii 91 One of the politest wits in the Kingdome for the Law. *a***1664** KATH. PHILIPS *To Abp. of Canterb.* Poems (1667) 166 Majestick sweetness, temper'd and refin'd, In a Polite and comprehensive Mind. **1711** ADDISON *Spect.* No. 39 ¶ 2 In all the polite Nations of the World, this part of the Drama has met with publick Encouragement. **1759** JOHNSON *Idler* No. 47 ¶ 14 Since his acquaintance with polite life. **1777** SIR W. JONES *Ess. Poetry E. Nat.* Poems, etc. 187 A very polite scholar, who has lately translated sixteen Odes of Hafez. **1840** MACAULAY *Ess., Ranke* (1851) II. 142 Whatever the polite and learned may think.

c. Of refined manners; *esp.* showing courteous consideration for others; courteous, mannerly, urbane. (The chief current use.)

1762 GOLDSM. *Cit. W.* xxxix, [He] perceives that the wise are polite all the world over, but that fools are polite only at home. **1772** MACKENZIE *Man World* II. xx. (1823) 492 The French are the politest enemies in the world. **1781** GIBBON *Decl. & F.* xix. II. 151 Narses .. was endowed with the most polite and amiable manners. **1807** CRABBE *Par. Reg.* III. 841 To them, to all, he was polite and free. **1831** SIR J. SINCLAIR *Corr.* II. 426 He sent me the following polite acknowledgment of his having received the work. **1856** 'Doing the polite' [see DO *v.* 11j]. **1883** *Manch. Guard.* 22 Oct. 5/5 Lord Dufferin obtains .. polite promises, but is not in a position to get anything more.

3. *absol.* or as *sb.* In colloq. phr, *to do the polite*: to perform a polite action (freq. with *thing* understood); to behave politely.

1856 [se do *v.* 11j]. **1933** D. L. SAYERS *Murder must Advertise* vi. 95, I saw you doing the polite to Miss Rossiter. **1935** G. GREENE *England made Me* iv. 199 They are leaving at the end of the week. I've got to do the polite. **1939** 'M. INNES' *Stop Press* i. vi. 136 Some chaps over there. Must do the polite.

[…]

politeness (pə(ʊ)ˈlaɪtnɪs). [f. as prec. + -NESS.] The quality of being polite.

† 1. *lit.* Polish, smoothness of surface. *Obs.*

1627 tr. *Bacon's Life & Death* (1651) 5 Smoothnesse, and Politenesse, of Bodies. **1669** GALE *Crt. Gentiles* I. III. iii. 47 Glasse is clear from its politenesse.

2. Mental or intellectual culture; polish, refinement, elegance, good taste (of writings, authors, etc.). Now *rare*.

1641 EVELYN *Diary* 28 Aug., The politeness of the character and editions of what he has publish'd. **1725** COTES tr. *Dupin's Eccl. Hist. 17th C.* I. v. 215 The Elegance and Politeness of the Stile of it. **1768** HUME *Ess., Civil Liberty* xi. 51 Dresden, not Hamburgh, is the centre of politeness in Germany. **1837–9** HALLAM *Hist. Lit.* I. i. i. §86. 78 In politeness of Latin style .. we find an astonishing and permanent decline both in France and England.

3. Polished manners, courtesy. Also as a mock title for people of polite manners.

1702 *Eng. Theophrast.* 108 Politeness may be defined a dextrous management of our Words and Actions whereby we make other people have better Opinion of us and themselves. **1735** J. THOMSON *Let.* 20 Oct. (in *Sotheby's Catal.* 19–22 Feb. (1896) 87) The gallant French this year have made war upon the Germans (I beg their Politeness's Pardon) like vermin — eat them up. **1757** SMOLLETT *Reprisal* I. i, The French will treat us with their usual politeness. **1802** MAR. EDGEWORTH *Moral T.* (1816) I. vii. 45 Real politeness only teaches us to save others from unnecessary pain. **1856** EMERSON *Eng. Traits, Aristocr.* Wks. (Bohn) II. 83 Politeness is the ritual of society, as prayers are of the church. **1875** JOWETT *Plato* (ed. 2) I. 207 If politeness would allow me I should say, Perish yourselves.[1]

Etymological dictionaries of German, such as the *Duden Etymologie* or *Kluge*, tell us that the abstract noun *Höflichkeit* is derived, as late as in the 15th century (Duden, *s.v.*), from the adj. *höflich*, which in turn is derived from German *Hof* and used to refer, together with *höfisch*, to the modes of life current at early modern *courts* (de.wiki[2]). *höfisch* and *höflich* both are calques from Old French *corteis*, which in turn is derived from Old French *co[u]rt* ("court," court of a principal; the principal and his entourage of noblemen,"Duden, *s.v.*). During the 12th century, *corteis* was taken over literally at first (as *kurteis*), then calqued as (mittelfränkisch) *hövesch, hüvesch* and (mittelhochdeutsch) *hüb[e]sch* (*ibid.*). As early as in the 13th century we encounter the verb *hofieren*, meaning at that time "to behave amiably and sociably, like at court, or to court, to serenade s.o."[3] (Kluge).

As a concept of its own, *Höflichkeit* thus emerged, during what Norbert Elias has called the "process of civilization," at the turn from the late Middle Ages to Modern Times, when the brutality and violence of the feudal nobility became tamed into the court nobility's *courtoisie* (de.

1 "polite" and "politeness" in the *Oxford English Dictionary*, 2nd ed.

2 Literally, "die Lebensart am frühneuzeitlichen Hof". <http://de.wikipedia.org/wiki/Höflichkeit> (accessed August 25, 2009).

3 "Sich gesellig (wie am Hof) verhalten, den Hof machen (frz. *faire la cour*), ein Ständchen darbringen". Kluge, 417, *s.v.* "hofieren".

wiki[4]), which, according to Elias, formed the first stage in the psychogenesis of modern man's personality, the next steps after *courtoisie* being the *civilité* of the courts during the period of monopolisation of the instruments of power and, after that, the *civilisation* (French) that accompanies the subsequent process of the socialisation and collectivisation of these monopolies.[5]

During the period of Humanism, the rules of conduct that had developed at court became increasingly identified, on the one hand, with Latin *civilitas* (which in itself was a translation of Greek πολιτεία[6] and had been in use since the 14th century, taken also into French as *civilité*); on the other hand it tended to merge, or increasingly overlap, with Latin *humanitas*. In this way, the polite manners of the courts came to be seen as modes of living that not only were opposed to non-urban barbarism, but were also believed to represent the only possible way of existence for a truly human being:

> court people, in whom *courtoisie* and *humanité* combined to what an Italian contemporary in 1528 termed *graziosa umanità*, actually claimed for themselves to be the only 'real' humans (*Geschichtliche Grundbegriffe* 3:1073-4). In the same way, also for Erasmus, e.g. in a treatise of 1530, *courtoisie* was almost equivalent to *civilitas*, and *civilitas* to *urbanitas* (7:697). For almost two centuries, *Höflichkeit* then remained a term with which rather 'uncourtly' concepts like *civilité*, which was Germanized only in pronunciation and ending (as *Civilitaet*), were rendered approximately (7:737).

With this, *Höflichkeit* gradually left the sphere of the court and 'descended,' down into the mundane and bourgeois spheres, only to spread over the whole of society a little later, so that, by the late 19th century, *any* citizen, no longer exclusively upper-class people or masters etc., was supposed to be addressed 'politely,' as a *Herr*.

In today's encyclopedias, finally, *Höflichkeit* has lost all 'courtly' connotations and is usually defined as a distanced, formal friendliness that aims at paying *respect*, *consideration* and *deference* towards the opposite

4 "[…] bei Hofe, wo die Rohheit und Gewalttätigkeit des *Feudaladels* zur höfischen Courtoisie des *Hofadels* gebändigt wurde": de.wiki (cf. above, fn. 2).

5 de.wikipedia.org/wiki/Über_den_Prozeß_der_Zivilisation (accessed August 25, 2009).

6 *Geschichtliche Grundbegriffe*, 7:696.

other,[7] and/or to recognize that other's social status[8] or, in one of the current politeness theories, as the expression of the speaker's intention to mitigate "face threats" carried by certain "face threatening acts" (FTA) toward another: "(...) the speaker avoids embarrassing the listener or making him feel uncomfortable."[9]

Be that is it may, the social rules and norms that a polite person conforms to and which are transmitted through *education* – the good manners or etiquette which give us a "polish" (cf. Latin *polītus* "polished" which is at the origin of French *poli* and English *polite*) – are considered mainly as a means to *prevent disturbances* of the social order which tactlessness and undisciplined egoism would provoke (de.wiki, summarizing the ideas of the German moral philosopher Friedrich Paulsen, 1846-1908).[10] So, the increasing self-restriction, the disciplining of egoism, and the internalisation of social norms which Norbert Elias described as characteristic of the European process of civilisation, the process that started with *courtoisie* and led to the formation of the Freudian super-ego (Über-Ich) in our personalities, – all this is still somehow contained in our contemporary concept of *Höflichkeit* or *politeness*.

———

Having looked at the etymology and semantic history of a concept of one or two Western languages and cultures, the same should be done now with the Arabic concepts which come to mind as closest renderings of the meaning of *Höflichkeit, politeness, politesse,* among them certainly *ʾadab* – as a quick look into some standard dictionaries suggests. Götz Schregle's German-Arabic dictionary (1974) gives:

höflich – I. (adj.) *muʾaddab, muhadhdhab;* ~es Lächeln *ibtisāmat al-mujāmala;* gegen j-n ~ sein *jāmala -hū, talaṭṭafa maʿa;* II. (adv.) *fī ʾadab, bi-luṭf;*

Höflichkeit – (des Benehmens) *ʾadab, taʾaddub, luṭf, liyāqa;* (die man sagt, erweist) *mujāmala;* j-m eine ~ erweisen *jāmala -hū;* aus ~ *bi-dāfiʿ al-ʾadab*[11]

7 "distanzierte, formale Freundlichkeit; Respekt von einer Person zu einer anderen": <http://de.wiktionary.org/wiki/Höflichkeit> (accessed August 28, 2009); "behaviour that is respectful and considerate of other people": *The Oxford Dictionary of English,* 2nd rev. ed., online version (accessed August 28, 2009 via <http://www.oxfordreference.com>, s.v. "polite".

8 <http://de.wikipedia.org/wiki/Höflichkeit> (accessed August 28, 2009).

9 <http://en.wikipedia.org/wiki/Politeness_theory> (accessed August 28, 2009).

10 <http://de.wikipedia.org/wiki/Höflichkeit> (accessed August 28, 2009).

11 Schregle 1974, s.v. [my transliteration, S.G.].

The online dictionary sakhr.com produces:

> **polite:** having or showing good manner: *ʾadīb, mutaʾaddib, khalūq, muʾaddab, mutarabb^{in}, murabb^{an}*
>
> **politeness:** quality of being polite: *ʾadab, taʾaddub, tahdhīb, luṭf*
>
> [French] **politesse:** ensemble des règles de savoir-vivre: *ʾadab, taʾaddub, talaṭṭuf, tahdhīb, dhawq, kiyāsa, labāqa, labaq, laṭāfa, luṭf, liyāqa, matānat al-khuluq*[12]

ʾadab or derivatives of the same root are mentioned in the front place in all these entries. This provides a kind of justification for me to focus on this term on the following pages though it is clear, of course, that *ʾ-d-b* is not the only root with a semantic value corresponding to *Höflich(keit)*, *polite(ness)*, etc., depending on what exactly is meant with the Western terms in a specific context. The focus on one single Arabic term and concept will however suffice, for the moment, to exemplify how a more comprehensive investigation, covering many more terms, could/should be carried out.

III – *ʾadab* – an Eastern concept

Whoever has a fair knowledge of Arabic will certainly have observed that the word *ʾadab* can take, and could take in the past, quite a variety of meanings. A roughly comprehensive overview over the modern uses of the term is given, for example, by the entry in *al-Muʿdjam al-wasīṭ*, which lists *four* basic meanings for the singular (plus a number of subdisciplines), and another *three* for the plural:

رياضة النفس بالتعليم والتهذيب على ما ينبغي . و- جملة ما ينبغي لذي الصناعة أو الفن أن يتمسك به ، كأَدب القاضي ، وأدب الكاتب . و- الجميل من النظم والنثر . و- كل ما أنتجه العقل الإنساني من ضروب المعرفة . وعلوم الأدب عند المتقدّمين تشمل : اللغة ، والصرف ، والاشتقاق ، والنحو ، والمعاني ، والبيان ، والبديع ، والعروض ، والقافية ، والخطّ ، والإنشاء ، والمحاضرات . (ج) **آداب** . وتطلق الآداب حديثاً على الأدب بالمعنى الخاصّ ، والتاريخ والجغرافية ، وعلوم اللسان والفلسفة . والآداب العامّة : العَرْف المقرَّر المَرْضِيّ . وآداب البحث والمناظرة : قواعد تبين وتنظّم كيفية المناظرة وشرائطها .[13]

---

12 <http://dictionary.sakhr.com> (accessed August 28, 2009) [my transliteration, S.G.].

13 *al-Muʿdjam al-wasīṭ*, I, 9 (*s.v.*).

In my (summary) translation:

sg. **ʾadab**

1) to train s.o., or discipline oneself (lit. the soul, *nafs*), through teaching and education in what is necessary, becoming, mandatory
2) all a craftsman or artist needs to observe [in his profession], e.g. the *ʾadab* of a judge, or of a scribe
3) beautiful poetry and prose
4) all kinds of knowledge the human mind has produced so far
5) There are also the *ʾadab* disciplines: *ʿilm al-lugha, al-ṣarf, al-ishtiqāq, al-naḥw, al-maʿānī, al-bayān, al-badīʿ, al-ʿarūḍ, al-qāfiya, al-khaṭṭ, al-ʾinshāʾ, al-muḥāḍarāt*

pl. **ʾādāb**

1) used recently for *ʾadab* in the narrower sense (i.e., literature), history and geography, linguistics and philosophy
2) common/general *ʾādāb*: generally acknowledged customs
3) *ʾādāb* in research and arguing: the rules/principles the show and govern/organize the way one argues and the premises on which the arguing rests

Similarly, but more concisely, the Arabic-English edition of Hans Wehr's dictionary summarizes:

[for the singular, *ʾadab*:] culture, refinement; good breeding, good manners, social graces, decorum, decency, propriety, seemliness; humanity, humaneness; the humanities; belles-lettres

[for the plural, *ʾādāb*:] decency, morals

The wide semantic spectrum displayed in this entry is not a recent development, however, as shows for instance Ahsan & Radspieler's *Lughāt-kitābı türkče–almanca / Türkisch-Arabisch-Deutsches Wörterbuch*, from the early 1910s.[14] For *ʾadab* it gives six major meanings:[15]

14 Tewfik Ahsan & E. A. Radspieler, لغات كتابى تركجه المانجه [*Lughāt-kitābı türkče–almanca*] / *Türkisch-Arabisch-Deutsches Wörterbuch*; Wien: Hartleben, [n.d.] (1911/12?).

15 English translation of German terms in brackets is mine, S.G. – Significantly, the German terms are in themselves not covered by one English term alone in most cases.

Erziehung	*Höflichkeit*	*Regel, Vorschrift*
(education, upbringing, educational background)	(politeness)	(rule, prescription, regulation)
Bildung	*gute Sitte*	*Literatur*
(education, erudition, formation, culture)	(good customs, conventions, manners)	(literature)

The situation was not less complex again almost a century earlier when Edward William Lane compiled his *Arabic-English Lexicon*, which builds on Murtaḍā al-Zabīdī's (d. 1205/1791) *Tāj al-ʿarūs*, which in turn reflects the semantic developments the term *ʾadab* had undergone until the 2nd half of the 18th century:

> ***ʾadab***, so termed because it invites men to the acquisition of praiseworthy qualities and dispositions, and forbids them from acquiring such as are evil, (T, Mgh,) signifies *Discipline of the mind;* and *good qualities and attributes of the mind* or *soul :* (Mṣb:) or *every praiseworthy discipline by which a man is trained in any excellence:* (AZ, Mgh, Mṣb :) [*good discipline of the mind and manners; good education; good breeding; good manners; politeness; polite accomplishments* :] *i.q.* ***ẓarf***[16] [as meaning *excellence,* or *elegance, of mind, manners, address, and speech*] : and *a good manner of taking or receiving* [what is given of offered or imparted, or what is to be acquired] : (M, A, Ḳ :) or *good qualities and attributes of the mind or soul,* and the *doing of generous* or *honourable actions :* (El-Jawáleeḳee :) or the *practice of what is praiseworthy both in words and actions :* or the *holding,* or *keeping, to those things which are approved, or deemed good ;* or the *honouring of those who are above one, and being gentle, courteous,* or *civil, to those who are below one :* (Towsheeḥ :) or *a faculty which preserves him in whom it exists from what would disgrace him :* (MF :) it is of two kinds, ***ʾadab al-nafs*** [which embraces all thc significations explained above], and ***ʾadab al-dars*** [which signifies *the discipline to be observed in the prosecution of study, by the disciple with respect to the preceptor, and be the preceptor with respect to the disciple:* see "Haji Khalfæ Lexicon," Vol. I. p. 212] : (Ṣ, Bṭl, Mgh:) [also *deportment,* or *a mode of conduct* or *behaviour,* absolutely; for one speaks of good ***ʾadab*** and bad ***ʾadab*** :] the pl. is ***ʾādāb*** [which is often employed, and so is the sing. also, as signifying the *rules of discipline to be observed in the exercise of a function,* such as that of a judge, and of a governor; and *in the exercise of an art,* such as that of the disputer, and

16 For this concept, cf. e.g. entry "Ẓarīf" (James E. Montgomery), in *Encyclopedia of Islam*, 2nd ed., vol. XI, 460, or article "Ẓarf" (Lois Giffen), in J. S. Meisami and P. Starkey (eds.), *Encyclopedia of Arabic Literature*, London 1998, ii, 821-822.

the orator, and the poet, and the scribe; &c.]. (Mṣb) — ***ʿilm al-ʾadab*** signifies [*The science of philology;* or] *the science by which one guards against error in the language of the Arabs, with respect to words and with respect ot writing;* ("Haji Khalfæ Lexicon," Vol. I. p. 215;) [and so, simply, ***al-ʾadab***: which is also used to signify *polite literature:* but in this sense, and likewise] as applied to *the sciences relating to the Arabic language,* [or *the philological sciences,* which is also termed ***al-ʿulūm al-ʾadabiyya,***] ***al-ʾadab*** is a post-classical term, innovated in the time of El-Islám. (El-Jawáleeḳee.) = ***ʾadab al-baḥr,*** (A, Ḳ,) or ***ʾadb al-baḥr,*** (T, L) *The abundance of water of the sea.* (T, A, L, Ḳ.)[17]

The *history of the concept,* i.e., the development that led to the large semantic variety of the term, has also been researched into quite extensively, and there is no need to repeat that in detail either. Practically all research in this field goes back to Nallino's seminal study of 1948,[18] the results of which have been summarized by Heribert Horst in *Grundriß der arabischen Philologie* (1987) as "Tradition → traditionelle (Herzens- und Verstandes-) Bildung → Bildung → Bildungsliteratur → Literatur,"[19] and the scruples Horst had in cutting down Nallino's findings to a simple scheme like this can be easily understood if one takes a look at Nallino's original tableau, which in itself is only a schematic illustration of his learned twenty-pages elaborations:

17 E. W. Lane, *An Arabic-English Lexicon*, i, 35. **Bold** = my transliteration from what in the dictionary is given in Arabic characters. For abbreviation of sources, see Lane's preface, part iv "Indications of Authorities," pp. xxxi-xiv.

18 First published in Carlo Alfonso Nallino, *Raccolta di scritti editi e inediti a cura di Maria Nallino*, vol. vi (Letteratura. Linguistica. Filosofia. Varia), Roma: Istituto per l'Oriente, 1948, 2-17.

19 "Die Entstehung der *adab*-Literatur und ihre Arten," in: Helmut Gätje (ed)., *Grundriß der Arabischen Philologie*, II: *Literaturwissenschaft*, Wiesbaden: Reichert, 208-220, here 208.

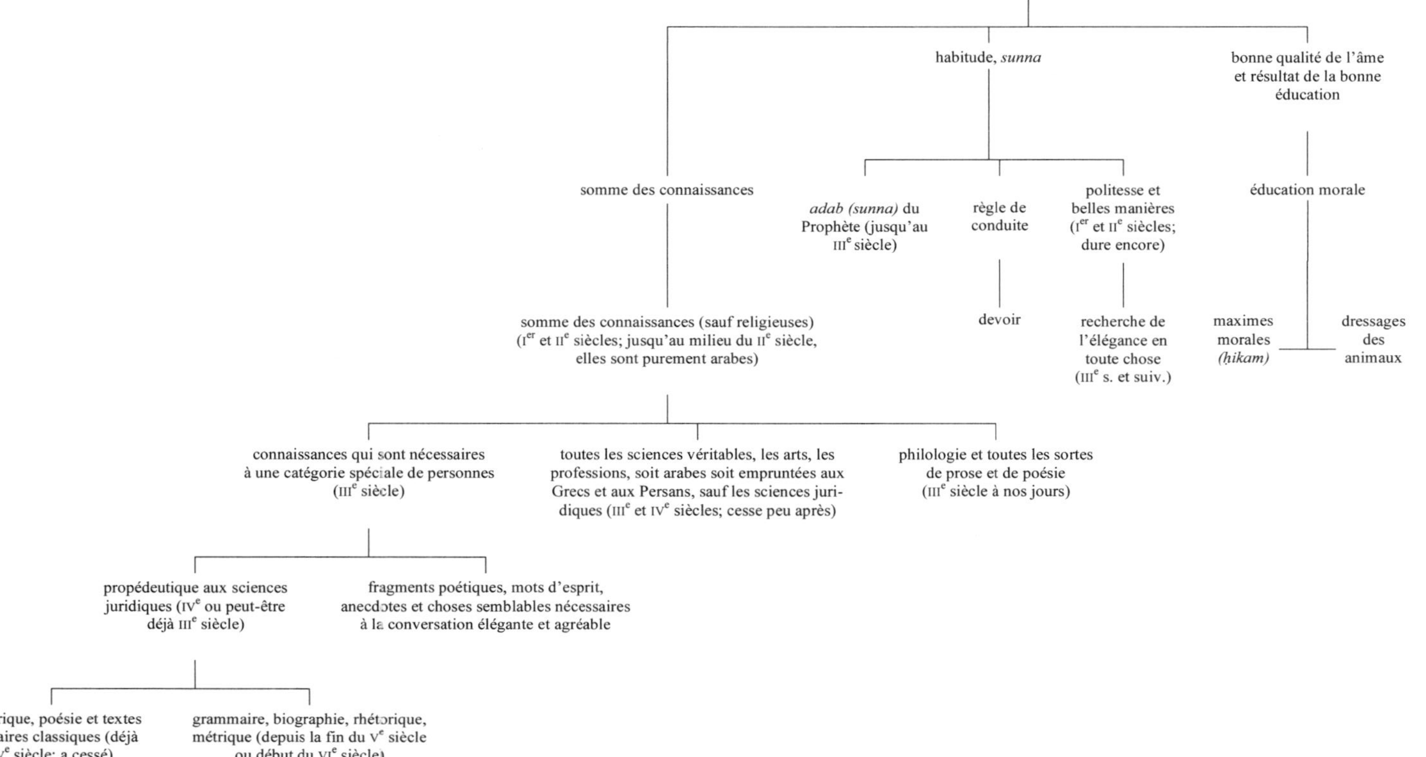
Habitudes héréditaires, *sunna*
somme des connaissances
habitude, *sunna*
bonne qualité de l'âme et résultat de la bonne éducation
adab (sunna) du Prophète (jusqu'au IIIe siècle)
règle de conduite
politesse et belles manières (Ier et IIe siècles; dure encore)
éducation morale
somme des connaissances (sauf religieuses) (Ier et IIe siècles; jusqu'au milieu du IIe siècle, elles sont purement arabes)
devoir
recherche de l'élégance en toute chose (IIIe s. et suiv.)
maximes morales (*ḥikam*)
dressages des animaux
connaissances qui sont nécessaires à une catégorie spéciale de personnes (IIIe siècle)
toutes les sciences véritables, les arts, les professions, soit arabes soit empruntées aux Grecs et aux Persans, sauf les sciences juridiques (IIIe et IVe siècles; cesse peu après)
philologie et toutes les sortes de prose et de poésie (IIIe siècle à nos jours)
propédeutique aux sciences juridiques (IVe ou peut-être déjà IIIe siècle)
fragments poétiques, mots d'esprit, anecdotes et choses semblables nécessaires à la conversation élégante et agréable
hétorique, poésie et textes ittéraires classiques (déjà IVe siècle; a cessé)
grammaire, biographie, rhétorique, métrique (depuis la fin du Ve siècle ou début du VIe siècle)

IV – Comparison

As mentioned above, a comparison between two cultures can be carried out on many levels and in many directions. One could, e.g., compare the *ways, techniques* and *linguistic devices* that are used in both cultures to show *Höflichkeit* or *politeness* on the one hand, or which kind of behaviour is to be expected from a *ʾadīb* or a *muʾaddab* or a *mutaʾaddib* on the other hand, or how *Höflichkeit / politeness* resp. *ʾadab* are expressed at certain times or in certain situations.[20] If one decides to go for a comparison of two *concepts*, each from a different language and culture, then the confrontation of *Höflichkeit / politeness* and *ʾadab*, which we have singled out for the purpose of this contribution, may produce results such as the following:

- The etymologies of the concepts of *politeness, Höflichkeit* and *ʾadab* point to different aspects of their origins. Whereas *politeness* is rendered as a quality (cf. the suffix *-ness*) that results from an *action*, the act of "polishing," smoothening, burnishing, i.e., whereas the English term originally stressed the process that necessarily precedes the achievement of that quality, German *Höflichkeit* related the concept to a social group and life-world: the court *(Hof)*.[21] In contrast, Arabic *ʾadab* etymologically neither points to an educational process nor a specific social environment, but rather (if it is really to be derived from the pl. of *daʾb* "custom") to the way of transmission of the necessary knowledge, to its being a kind of imitation, of continuing a tradition of approved customs.[22]
- The subsequent development of the concepts is of course very complex and therefore difficult to compare. Yet, it can be said that what the German and English concepts as well as the Arabic counterpart have in common is the fact that for each of them the appropriation and incorporation of foreign elements, the assimilation to models

20 Under the heading "Techniques to show politeness" the English *wikipedia* mentions: hedging and indirectness; polite lying; use of euphemism (incl. ambiguity & connotation); preference of tag questions to direct statements; modal tags; affective tags, incl. softeners; facilitative tags. See <http://en.wikipedia.org/wiki/Politeness> (accessed December 4, 2008).

21 See above, pp. 10–13.

22 See above, pp. 15ff.

encountered in Iran resp. in France, have become crucial.[23] After the contact with the foreign culture, both *Höflichkeit* and *ʾadab* (these two at least – I don't know whether *politeness* would have to be included as well) come to signify the ethos of a certain social elite – the court on the one hand, the class of *kuttāb* (scribes, secretaries) on the other –, and from there, it undergoes an amplification, a broadening into the meaning of a general *humanitas*. Both concepts have a number of components in common:

- They have an *intellectual* aspect: both require a certain amount of *knowledge* (although, in the case of modern *Höflichkeit*, this is the knowledge only of some rules of conduct and good manners, whereas a *ʾadīb*, and perhaps even a person described as *muʾaddab* or *mutaʾaddib*, will know much more than a person who is just *höflich*).
- Both terms have an *educational* component: *Höflichkeit* presupposes some learning and training, an aspect which today is most strongly preserved in the Arabic form II (*ʾaddaba, taʾdīb*).
- Both can also signify *ethical* concepts (cf. the definition as *riyāḍat al-nafs* "discipline of the mind," character, intention, in *al-Muʿjam al-wasīṭ* quoted above), an ethos which is connected with discipline and self-restriction, a "process of civilization."
- Both are *normative*, comprise a set of formalaties and rules of conduct: cf., e.g., the "rules of *Höflichkeit*" and the Arabic *ʾadab* manuals.
- Both are, at a certain period, *class* concepts and refer to an elite of superior education. Much of this connotation has been lost during

23 For *Höflichkeit* cf. the steps mentioned above, pp. 12–14. As for Arabic, a number of studies illustrate the 'contamination' of the original Arabic meaning through foreign, esp. Persian, models by pointing to a passage by Ibn Sahl (d. 236/850-851), who differentiates between ten 'disciplines' of *ʾadab*, only three of them being of Arab(ic) origin (*shiʿr* "poetry," *nasab* "genealogy," and *ʾayyām al-nās* "history/biography [?]"), while playing the lute, chess, and polo as well as medicine, mathematics/geometry, and *furūsiyya* [riding?, hippology?] are traced back to Persian origins. Superior to all of these, Ibn Sahl says, is the art of storytelling and good entertainment in evening gatherings. Quoted by Abū Isḥāq Ibrāhīm b. ʿAlī al-Ḥuṣrī al-Qayrawānī in the chapter on "al-muḥādatha wa'l-mujālasa" of his *Zahr al-ʾādāb wa-thamr al-ʾalbāb* [comp. 405/1014-5], ed. ʿAlī Muḥ. al-Bidjāwī, [Cairo:] Dār ʾIḥyāʾ al-kutub al-ʿarabiyya / ʿĪsā al-Bābī al-Ḥalabī, ṭ. 2 , [n.d.], p. 155. – Cf. Goldziher 1913.

the process of generalization in both cases. But at least *Höflichkeit* has retained the social aspect, although it is less class than social *status* in general which matters, the respect one owes one's counterpart because of age, sex, social standing, etc., i.e. there is an element of power resp. powerlessness/impotence involved – which, I think, is absent from *ʾadab* (in most cases at least).

- Among the major differences between the two concepts today one could mention the following:
  - In the case of *ʾadab*, there is an intimate connection with literacy, scriptuality, and literature, which seems to be missing in the modern usage of *Höflichkeit* although education has been constitutive for some time.
  - The gestures, linguistic devices etc., with which politeness is expressed may differ considerably from culture to culture (an aspect we have not had a closer look at above).
  - Although *ʾadab* also signifies, according to the Arab lexicographers, a "discipline of the mind," i.e. it necessitates a kind of "taming" of the *nafs*, I think this taming is not the same as the increasing restriction of the self and of egoistic instincts which Norbert Elias described as the "process of civilisation" and which, according to him, lead to a gradual internalization of norms and rules within western personality and to the emergence of the Freudian "super-ego." There is, it seems, no connection of *ʾadab* in Arabic with an "Über-Ich" (whatever this might be in Arabic).[24]
  - This may have something to do with another difference. On many instances, the self-restriction associated with German *Höflichkeit* leads to a merely *formal* conduct which conceals the ever-virulent libidinous drives or other rather impolite impulses and is therefore equated, since the times of Enlightenment, with insincerity, falseness, lying, dissimulation, or hypocrisy. Enlightenment being the movement mainly of the emerging bourgeoisie, this class accused the ruling nobility, most prominent among them the rulers and their entourage, the people of the court, of being false

24 Cf. the interesting article by Oddbjørn Leirvik on "Conscience in Arabic and the Semantic History of *ḍamīr*," *Journal of Arabic and Islamic Studies*, 9/2 (2009): 18-36, accessible online under <http://www.lancs.ac.uk/jais/volume/docs/vol9/v9_2_Leirvik_18-36.pdf>.

and associated court life and its modes of conduct with falseness, while they claimed for themselves to be the only garantee of sincerity and true, good morals. An echo of this equation can be found in J. W. Goethe's (1749-1832) *Faust*, part II (completed 1831), where the *baccalaureus* says that in German, to be polite means to tell lies ("Im Deutschen lügt man, wenn man höflich ist"[25]).

– In contrast, neither does the concept of *ʾadab* nor polite behaviour towards others in general have any such connotations in an Arab (ic) context. The indigenous etymology may not be scientifically correct; from a cultural perspective, however, it seems to be not without significance that Arab lexicographers relate *ʾadab* to the verb *ʾadaba* "to invite (to a repast, a banquet, i.e. a *maʾduba*)":[26] the first explanation Lane quotes on the authority of the *Tahdhīb* of al-Azharī (282-370/1 H. / 895-980 C.E.) and the *Mughrib* of al-Muṭarrizī (536-610 H. / 1144-1213 C.E.) is that *ʾadab* is termed *ʾadab* "because it *invites* men to the acquisition of praiseworthy qualities and dispositions, and forbids them from acquiring such as are evil."[27] That is, the term stresses the *positive* aspects rather than implying just a suppression or veiling of morally unseemly aspirations. Its function is rather, as Asfa-Wossen Asserate, an Ethiopian prince who grew up and studied in Germany, put it, to comply with our fellow human beings' need for esteem and being spared direct confrontation with the unpleasant aspects of the world.[28] He says:

> "Manieren sind das Parfüm, das vergessen läßt, daß wir stinken […]. Das ästhetische Bedürfnis, dessen Ergebnis das 'uneigentliche Sprechen' des Orients … ist, hat mit Betrug und Verfälschung der Wirklichkeit nichts zu tun, denn es setzt die rückhaltlose Kenntnis der Wirklichkeit voraus; man könnte sagen, seine Funktion ist die des Trostes über die Welt, wie sie nun einmal ist."
>
> "Good manners are the perfume which lets us forget that we are stinking. […] The aesthetic impulse that produces the Orient's 'tropical discourse' has nothing to do with deceit or the adulteration of reality, since it pre-

---

25 Act II, "Hochgewölbtes, enges, gotisches Zimmer," v. 6771.

26 Cf. Lane, *Arabic-English Lexicon*, i, 34. – Wehr (English): "to invite (to a party or a banquet […])", *ʾadaba maʾdubatan* "to arrange a banquet, give a formal dinner".

27 Lane, *Arabic-English Lexicon*, i, 35 (my italics, S.G.).

28 Asfa-Wossen Asserate, *Manieren*, Frankfurt a.M.: Eichborn-Verlag, 2003 (Die Andere Bibliothek), 75.

> supposes a pitiless knowledge of that reality; one could rather say, its function is that of a consolation over the world as we know it is."[29]

V – Research lacunas

What I have presented so far may, in spite of its conciseness, look quite comprehensive, or at least give the impression to have the potential to be comprehensive. Yet, as Arabic is concerned, this is by far not the case, and much of what I have said about *ʾadab* until now rests on a rather unstable ground. Compared to German or English, Arabic conceptual history is still a rather underresearched field.

To take *ʾadab* again as an example, this concept may seem to have been covered satisfactorily already by the studies of Nallino 1948, Pellat 1964, and Bonebakker 1990 (to name only the most prominent); but

1) these (and other) studies differ from each other in quite a number of details, as is already clear from Pellat's modifications to Nallino's findings, and again from Susan Bonebakker's reservations against both Nallino and Pellat.[30]
2) Practically all of them are very imprecise as to the chronology of the semantic changes they observe. If we deal with dictionaries, they may be quite comprehensive and even give quotes from the sources, but their approach usually is rather additive than historically systematic and tends to ignore the chronology of the semantic changes that can be observed. If the sources are given, and if they can be considered authentic, these may be brought into chronological order on the user's own initiative (as, e.g., in Lane), but in order to reach a result like that of the entries in the *Oxford English Dictionary* (see Table 1 above), an enormous effort is needed.
3) Only rarely do they attempt to locate such changes in the cultural context and in this way give explanations as to why the meaning of a concept may have changed at a given time in history.[31]
4) All of them are rather impressionistic studies, they do not rest upon a *systematic* approach to the sources. Sources for assumptions or assertions are often not given, chronologies left incomplete and thus

29 Asserate 2003, 74-75 (my English, S.G.).

30 Cf. Bonebakker 1990, 16f.

31 To a certain degree, this lacuna is filled by the entries in the *Encyclopedia of Islam*, however deficient they may be as far as the other aspects are concerned.

semantic transitions unexplained or, at best, undocumented, not bothering about finding the missing links, etc.

5) Despite some glances at Western correspondences, none of these studies has a thorough and systematic culturally comparative approach.

A quick glance at only one aspect of conceptual history, the *etymology* of the term *ʾadab*, may suffice to illustrate my point. In spite of numerous studies on the term and concept, its etymology still remains rather vague. The *ʾadab* we are dealing with here does not seem to have any real cognates in other Semitic languages. Hebrew *ʾadīb* "faire languir, faire dépérir" (to let die off, or shrink, to weaken, or make slacken, to let or make shrivel, or disrupt s.th.) and Soqotri *ʾidbeh* "pied de devant" (front leg/foot), which David Cohen lists in his *Dictionnaire des racines semitiques* (1970 ff.),[32] would seem quite difficult to relate semantically to the meaning *ʾadab* appears with in the oldest Arabic sources, namely that of "'habit, hereditary norm of conduct, custom' derived from ancestors and other persons who are looked up to as models (as, in the religious sense, was the *sunna* of the Prophet for his community)" (Gabrieli 1960/2008).[33] With this meaning, it has a parallel in Tigre, where *'adab* means, among other – probably later – meanings, also "habitude" (Cohen); but at least this form, Cohen says, "est un emprunt direct à l'arabe" (is a direct loan from Arabic). A connection to the verb *ʾadaba* meaning "to invite," which Arab lexicographers usually assume and which shows a counterpart in Soqotri *ʾdb* "to invite" and perhaps also in Amharic *ağğäbä* "faire escorte à qu. pour le rendre honneur" (to accompany s.o. in order to pay honour him), seems rather unlikely, so that the notorious etymology put forward by Nallino – "that the plural *ādāb* was formed from *daʾb* ('custom, habit'), and that the singular *adab* was subsequently derived from this plural" (Gabrieli 1960/2008) – does not seem completely implausible. All the more so since Ilse Lichtenstädter's cautious proposal to link Arabic *ʾadab* to a Sumerian *é-dub-ba-a,* signifying "school" or "university,"[34] seems rather far-fetched (to say the least), and Asya Asbaghi's tracing Arabic *ʾadab* to a – or rather two – earlier (!) Persian *adab*s which go back to two Middle Persian expressions, is motivated too obviously by Iranian patriotism as to pass critical

32 s.v. "'DB, -2. can." resp. "'DB, -3. sar.".

33 Entry "Adab" in the *Encyclopedia of Islam,* 2nd ed., vol. i.

34 Lichtenstädter 1974, quoted by Horst 1987, 208.

checking.[35] (It may suffice here to note that the Persian term *adab* does not appear in Persian sources earlier than 325/936).[36]

But even if there is no *direct* borrowing from the Persian lexicon, the semantic development of the Arabic words for "good old customs, praiseworthy habits" into the whole later concept of *ʾadab* has certainly been influenced, if not essentially shaped, by Iranians. It is probably not wrong to follow the entry in *Encyclopedia Iranica* (1985) here, which says that "[t]he origin of the concept can be traced to pre-Islamic and especially Sasanian Iran,"[37] and that it is, the moment it appears in Persian sources, "the equivalent of the Middle Persian *frahang* and New Persian *farhang*,"[38] although the coming of Islam had by then already "added to it many new elements and brought about a specifically Islamic synthesis."[39]

If in the beginning *ʾadab* was more or less synonymous with *sunna*,[40] and if it is no lexical borrowing, then the question arises why a new expression was coined by forming a new singular from a plural that meant "customs, habits, wont." A possibility I would suggest is that it was a calque for Persian *ēwēn* (New Persian *āyīn*) which means "custom, rule, correct manner, and the like"[41] and for the Arabs must have seemed something different from their own *sunan* and *ʾadʾub* (another plural of *daʾb*). The fact that after the rise of Islam the term *sunna* came to refer, more and more exclusively, to the Prophet's exemplary manners and way of life and thus acquired a religious connotation, produced a need to have a term for the secular tradition.

35 Asbaghi 1988 has two entries for *ʾadab*. The first *ʾadab*, meaning "gute Sitten, Anstand, Höflichkeit" (good manners, consideration, politeness), is traced back to Persian *adab* and *āyīn*, both of which are said to have Middle Persian *aīvēn* as their ancestor, which in turn goes back, allegedly, to an Old Iranian **abi-dagna*. The second meaning, "literarische Bildung" (literary formation, knowledge of/from literature) is seen as a loanword from another, equally earlier (!) Persian *adab*, which, Asbaghi thinks, goes back via Middle Persian *dipi* "Inschrift" (inscription) to Old Iranian **dipi-vara*.

36 Khaleghi-Motlagh, "Adab: i. Adab in Iran," *Encyclopedia Iranica*, i, 432.

37 Khaleghi-Motlagh 1985, 431.

38 *Ibid.*, 432.

39 *Ibid.*, 431.

40 The question why this should be the case, i.e., why we should assume that there were two different terms for nearly the same meaning, remains open.

41 Khaleghi-Motlagh, 432.

But – does the Arab singular *ʾadab* really not appear earlier than at the time of the early Islamic expansion? No reliable sources can answer this question.

VI – EDALC

In order to fill the above mentioned lacunas, or at least to contribute to this task, the project of an *Etymological Dictionary of Arabic Language and Culture* (EDALC) has been launched. EDALC is planned as an electronic database (Internet portal) that highlights Arab cultural history through the semantic history of the vocabulary of the Arabic language, concentrating, for the time being, on terms of particular significance, such as modes of living or cultural techniques, as well as on key concepts of religion, philosophy, society, politics, etc. It is meant to be a field of co-operation and synergy of experts from various disciplines, especially linguists (Arabists, Semiticists, Afroasiaticists in the first place, but naturally also Iranists, Graeco-Romanists, etc.) and cultural historians, but of course also colleagues with an expertise in related disciplines, like the political, social, economic, religious history of the Middle East, as well as the history of sciences, esp. botany, pharmacology, chemistry, astronomy; archaeological and genetic findings will also become relevant.

Since EDALC does not start from point zero in any of these fields – a fact that not only the above example of *ʾadab* testifies to –, one of the project's major tasks will be to collect, bundle and process the huge amount of already existing material. On the other hand, as the example of *ʾadab* likewise has demonstrated rather clearly, this process itself will make those areas apparent where additional research is needed.

The length of the time period covered and the diversity of spheres of life touched by EDALC make it a large-scale project which will not only involve a large number of scholars from a great variety of research fields, but will also operate on a long-term basis as an international joint-venture. Wherever possible, EDALC will profit from possibilities of synergy with ongoing overlapping projects (e.g., projects on the vocabulary of the Qurʾān). Part and parcel of these synergies will also be, as a matter of course, connecting to online databases and thesauri as well as lexico-statistical projects.

The form of publication through which EDALC is thought to be made accessible – a web-based platform / internet portal – will guarantee open access to all information and the possibility to contribute for everybody worldwide. Bearing this 'openness' and publicity in mind, the entries will provide summaries alongside the long, detailed academic essays. Each entry consists of an Arabic word/concept, its etymology in concise form (tracing it back to earlier forms and giving cognates in other languages, indicating changes of meaning etc.), then explaining the findings with reference to their background, e.g., the transfer of a term from Greek via Aramaic in the course of the great translation movements, or the adoption of a cultural technique from the Persians, or the coining of a new term from an Arabic root under the conditions of a changed environment, or the modification of meaning of existing words in order to express new concepts, etc. For all data, references will be given, and the context of the original will be provided as a quote from the sources consulted. Besides the full academic entry a 'light' version may be produced if necessary/advisable. This 'popular' version is meant to provide the interested 'lay' public with research-based, yet easily accessible and 'digestable' expertise on the historical and cultural background of, among others, terminological key-concepts that have become known, and may even be commonplace, in the West (as, e.g., *jihād, sharīʿa, fidāʾī*, etc.) but are often misunderstood and interpreted out of context. EDALC will however also be searchable in the opposite direction: there will not only be an entry on *ʾadab*, for example, but also on *politeness* and/or *Höflichkeit*, that paves the way for a comparative approach. Entries on Arabic as well as on English terms/concepts will be crossreferenced in order to facilitate comparison across the cultures.

For the time being, EDALC is planned to concentrate on *fuṣḥā* (although using relevant findings of dialectology) and on only a limited number of selected roots and terms. During the start-up phase it will also be focussing on vocabulary in present-day use only. A number of entries to start with have been selected.

Bibliography

Ahsan, Tewfik / Radspieler, E. A. (1911/12?): لغات كتابى تركجه المانجه [*Lughāt-kitābı türkče–almanca*] / *Türkisch-Arabisch-Deutsches Wörterbuch*. Hartleben, Wien [n.d.].

Asbaghi, Asya (1988): *Persische Lehnwörter im Arabischen*. Harrassowitz, Wiesbaden.

Asserate, Asfa-Wossen (2003): *Manieren*. Eichborn-Verlag, Frankfurt a.M. (Die Andere Bibliothek)

Bonebakker, Susan A. (1990): "*Adab* and the Concept of Belles-Lettres". In: [*The Cambridge History of Arabic Literature –] ʿAbbasid Belles-Lettres*, ed. Julia Ashtiany et al., Cambridge University Press, 16-30.

Cohen, David (1970 ff.): *Dictionnaire des racines semitiques ou attestées dans les langues sémitiques, comprenant un ficher comparatif de Jean Cantineau*. Peeters, [Leuven] / Mouton, Paris.

DUDEN Etymologie. Herkunftswörterbuch der deutschen Sprache (1963). Bearbeitet von Günther Drosdowski, Paul Grebe [et al.]. Bibliographisches Institut, Mannheim/ Zürich. (Der große Duden; 7).

EALL see *Encyclopedia of Arabic Language and Linguistics*.

EI see *Encyclopedia of Islam*.

Encyclopedia of Arabic Language and Linguistics [EALL] / general editor Kees Versteegh; ass. editors Mushira Eid ... [et al.]. Leiden: Brill, 2006-2009.

The Encyclopedia of Islam, 2nd ed. [EI^2] / ed. P. Bearman [et al.]. Leiden: Brill, 1960-2009.

Fähndrich, Hartmut (1990): "Der Begriff 'adab' und sein literarischer Niederschlag". In: *Neues Handbuch der Literaturwissenschaft*, vol. 5: *Orientalisches Mittelalter*, ed. Wolfhart Heinrichs et al., AULA-Vlg., Wiesbaden, 326-345.

Gabrieli, Francesco (2008): "Adab." In: *Encyclopaedia of Islam*, 2nd ed. Brill, Leiden. Online version. [Original printed version 1960].

Geschichtliche Grundbegriffe. Historisches Lexikon zur politisch-sozialen Sprache in Deutschland, ed. Otto Brunner, Werner Conze, Reinhart Koselleck. Klett-Cotta, Stuttgart. Vol. 3 (1982), vol. 7 (1992).

Goldziher, Ignac (1913): "Adab." In: *Enzyclopädie des Islams*, 1st ed. Brill, Leiden, vol. 1, 129-130.

Horst, Heribert (1987): "Die Entstehung der adab-Literatur und ihre Arten". In: *Grundriß der arabischen Philologie*, vol. II: *Literaturwissenschaft*, ed. Helmut Gätje, L. Reichert, Wiesbaden, 208-220.

[al-Ḥuṣrī:] Abū Isḥāq Ibrāhīm b. ʿAlī al-Ḥuṣrī al-Qayrawānī: *Zahr al-ʾādāb wa-t͟hamr al-ʾalbāb* [comp. 405/1014-5], ed. ʿAlī Muḥammad al-Bid͟jāwī. [Cairo:] Dār ʾIḥyāʾ al-kutub al-ʿarabiyya / ʿĪsā al-Bābī al-Ḥalabī, ṭ. 2 , [n.d.].

Khaleghi-Motlagh, Dj. (1985): "Adab: i. Adab in Iran". In: *Encyclopedia Iranica*, ed. Ehsan Yarshater, vol. i, Routledge & Kegan Paul, London etc., 431-39.

Kluge. Etymologisches Wörterbuch der deutschen Sprache, bearb. von Elmar Seebold. Berlin & New York: Walter de Gruyter, ^{24}2002.

Lane, Edward William (1863): *An Arabic-English Lexicon*, vol. I. London: Williams and Norgate. Reprint Beirut: Librairie du Liban, 1968.

Leirvik, Oddbjørn (2009): "Conscience in Arabic and the Semantic History of *ḍamīr*." *Journal of Arabic and Islamic Studies*, 9/2: 18-36, accessible online under <http://www.lancs.ac.uk/jais/volume/docs/vol9/v9_2_Leirvik_18-36.pdf>.

Lichtenstädter, Ilse (1974): *Introduction to Classical Arabic Literature*. Twayne, New York.

al-Muʿdjam al-wasīṭ, ed. Ibrāhīm Muṣṭafā, Ḥāmid ʿAbd al-Qādir, Aḥmad Ḥasan al-Zayyāt, Muḥammad al-Naḏjḏjār. al-Maktaba al-ʿilmiyya, Ṭahrān [n.d.].

Nallino, Carlo-Alfonso (1950 [1948]): "Sens pris par le mot *adab* aux divers siècles". In: id., *La littérature arabe des origines à l'époque de la dynastie umayyade. Leçons professées en arabe à l'Université du Cairo.* Traduction française par Charles Pellat d'après la version italienne de Maria Nallino [Roma 1948], Paris: Maisonneuve, 1950 (Islam d'hier et d'aujourd'hui; 6), 7-28.

The Oxford English Dictionary, 2nd ed. (1989), prepared by J. A. Simpson & E. S. C. Weiner. Claredon Pr., Oxford (vol. XII Poise-Quelt).

Pellat, Charles (1964): "Variations sur le thème de l'adab." *Correspondance d'Orient, Études* 5-6: 19-37.

Schregle, Götz (1974): *Deutsch-Arabisches Wörterbuch*. Wiesbaden: Harrassowitz.

Shivtiel, Avihai (2008): "Politeness". In: *EALL*, vol. 3, 658-663.

Wehr, Hans (1966): *A Dictionary of Modern Written Arabic*, ed. J. Milton Cowan, Harrassowitz, Wiesbaden (2nd printing).

Wehr, Hans (1998): *Arabisches Wörterbuch für die Schriftsprache der Gegenwart. Arabisch–deutsch.* 5th ed. Harrassowitz, Wiesbaden.

http://de.wikipedia.org/wiki/Höflichkeit

http://de.wikipedia.org/wiki/Über_den_Prozeß_der_Zivilisation

http://de.wiktionary.org/wiki/höflich

http://de.wiktionary.org/wiki/Höflichkeit

http://dictionary.sakhr.com/

http://en.wikipedia.org/wiki/Politeness

http://en.wikipedia.org/wiki/Politeness_theory

http://en.wikipedia.org/wiki/The_Civilizing_Process

Language and Mentality: Politeness, Courtesies and Gestures in Palestinian Arabic

Avihai Shivtiel, Cambridge

This article is dedicated to the memory of my late mother from whom I had learned all this and much more.

Mentality is generally defined as a way of thinking, behaviour and attitudes of the individual or those shared by a group of people. These may be concluded from his or their reactions and actions as well as from the language used by the individual or by the society at large. Hence, although any generalisation concerning certain characteristics of a community may result in undesirable bias and often dangerous stereotyping, the language and style used by the individual or by the community can often reflect positive as well as negative distinctive characteristic features.

Politeness is a norm of social behaviour that reflects endearment, respect, esteem and much more, towards another person or towards a group of people. It is usually associated with the language used on various occasions and in different circumstances, as well as the use of voice, intonation, gestures and courtesies – all are said to show good manners and refined upbringing.

This paper will attempt to analyse some phrases and expressions that are used by speakers of the Palestinian dialects, as part of their code of behaviour, demonstrating often politeness and courtesy. However, since some of the phrases also exist in other Arabic dialects, these characteristics may indeed go beyond the boundaries of the Palestinian linguistic milieu. It will also attempt at reaching some conclusions regarding common features, which reflect customs and manners and even what may be called the mentality of the society under discussion.

Let us examine now some of the main characteristics as reflected in some common phrases and expressions. However, before we do so we have to bear in mind that the following examples are by no means comprehensive as they have been selected from a much bigger collection of examples current in the Palestinian dialects,[*] most of which I had learned from my late mother, Mrs Margalit Shivtiel, née Antebi (1910–2003), who was born in Safad in Palestine.

1. A Strong belief in and complete devotion to God

A cursory look at the large stock of expressions widely used in daily communication proves the existence of hundreds, if not of thousands of phrases which contain the name of God,[1] the commonest being: *al-ḥamdu li-llāh* – praise to God, *allāhu ʾakbar* – God is the greatest, *bi-smi llāhi r-raḥmāni r-raḥīm* – in the name of Allah the Compassionate the Merciful, *ʾinšallah* – God willing, *allāhu ʾaʿlam* – God alone knows, *ʾaʿūzu bi-llāh, lā samaḥa llāh* – God forbid, and many more. Moreover, some expressions may be used in more than one situation, e.g., *smallah ʿalēk* – may God protect you from the evil eye (often used in reaction to good behaviour of a child) is an expression which may also be used sarcastically meaning "you don't say!", and *lā ʾilāha ʾillā llāh* – used as a spontaneous reaction on hearing bad news, or to express one's surprise.

Moreover, the name *allāh* may even be used on its own as an invocation to God, while it may also render a different meaning distinguished only by intonation, e.g., *allāh!* [in an affirmative tone] used in calming a person, usually a child, who e.g., has stumbled and knocked his foot etc. or is coughing heavily, while *allāh?* [in an interrogative tone] is usually used to express surprise. The same can be said about the phrase *wallāh(i)* [in the affirmative] meaning "I swear by God" and *wallāh(i)?* [in the interrogative tone], meaning "Is it true? Are you sure?", or, *yā allāh* – often used to express impatience or surprise, e.g., *yā allāh! ʾēmta raḥ yexalleṣ*? My God, when is he going to finish? or, *šūf, šūf!! yā allāh* – Look! Look! My God! Similarly, the expression *yā rabb* may be used as an invocation to God or may also be used as an indication of impatience, e.g., *yā rabb, ʿaṭīna l-quwwe* – Please, God, give us the strength, or *yā rabb, kafa!* God, (it's) enough!

---

* Editorial note: not all of the examples are transcribed in a strictly dialectal fashion, as some examples constitute borrowings from Classical Arabic in the respective dialects. In our editing, *hamzat al-qaṭʿ* is transcribed, while *hamzat al-waṣl* is not, even though a glottal stop may be audible here and there.

1 See Piamenta 1983: 1.

2. Self-Honour

Honour, dignity and self-respect are 'sacred' concepts among Arabs since pre-Islamic times, and are considered taboos, which should not be abused by anybody. Moreover, the honour of the self, the family and the clan should be protected at all cost, as it is more important than life. Hence, revenge is an inevitable practice to save honour.[2]

The words *ʿarḍ, šaraf, karāme, ḥaḍra, iḥtirām, bayāḍ al-wušš* and their derivatives mean honour and respect, and are used extensively in daily intercourse. E.g., *bi-ʿarḍak, bi-šarafi* – by your / my honour, usually used in oaths or for emphasising the truth of a claim; *šarrfūna* – honour us, is a common invitation to guests, like *tšarrafnā* – we are honoured, as a polite way of accepting one; *tikram* (lit. "you are respected"), (approx.) your wish is my command; *šū ism al-karīm* or *šū ism ḥaḍrtak* (lit. what is the name of your honour), i.e. what is your name?

Popular expressions, stressing readiness to give services, are: *karmal liḥyatak / daqnak* – (lit. "out of respect to your beard") or *karmal ʿēnak* – (lit. out of respect to your eye), all meaning 'I'll do it with pleasure', 'at your service', and *iḥtirāmi, yā sīdi* – (lit. "my respect for you, Sir"), i.e. 'yes, sir', when addressing a superior, and many more.

The attitude to females and the position of women in Arab society is the subject of ongoing debate, which is beyond the scope of this paper. However, the general attitude, which springs from the concern about the honour of the family, can be concluded from some of the popular expressions used. Thus, it is certainly humiliating to name a father of girls *ʾabū banāt* – father of girls. The custom is to address both parents after their son, e.g., *ʾabū / ʾumm muḥammad* instead of using their first names, but only a mother may be addressed as 'the mother of' followed by her daughter's name, e.g., *ʾumm maryam*. Moreover, when the first born is a female, one of the customary congratulations at birth is *tkūn ʾuxt sabʿ banīn* – may she be the sister of seven boys. So far as other females in the family are concerned, they may be approached as 'the mother of ...' or *ʾuxti* – my sister, *bint ʿammi / xālti* – my aunt, or sitt ... (Mrs. ...). In inquiring about the health of a wife of a person, who is not a close member

2 The pre-Islamic custom of blood-revenge is deeply rooted in Arab society. See also Qurʾān 5:45. The commitment of taking revenge is clearly illustrated by the famous proverb: *baʿd arbʿīn sana ʾaxad al-badawi taʾro* – the Bedouin has taken his revenge after forty years. Cf. also Lane, p. 120, where he discusses the issue of blood revenge among Bedouins.

of the family, one must refer to her as *al-ʾahl* – the family or *ʾumm al-wilād* – the mother of the children, e.g., *kīf ḥāl al-ʾahl?* – how is the family? or *kīf ḥāl ʾumm al-wilād?* – how is the mother of the children? An enquiry about a daughter is *kīf ḥāl al-karīme?* – how is the respected one?, i.e. your daughter.

An interesting case in the context of honour are the words 'shoes', 'dog' and 'donkey' which are taboos, and are considered offensive. Hence, they should be avoided in daily communication. However, if reference must be made to them in a conversation, a parenthetical phrase may precede or follow them, showing respect for the addressee. The commonest phrases are *ʾajallak* – (lit. "you are more elevated / respected than this one") or *baʿīd ʿannak* – (lit. "far from you"), e.g., *štarēt mbāriḥ baʿīd ʿannak / ʾajallak kundra* – I bought yesterday – far from you / you are more respected – shoes. *Yūsuf ʾilo fi l-mazraʿa ʾajallak / baʿīd ʿannak ʿišrīn ḥmār u-kalb* – Joseph has in the farm – far from you – twenty donkeys and a dog. *Šuft ibn al-kalb – ʾajallak / baʿīd ʿannak – šū sawa fīna?* – did you see what this son of a bitch – far from you / you are more respected – has done to us?[3]

3. Strong belief in superstitions

Similar to other societies Arab society strongly believes in superstitions. Hence, the Devil, jinns, demons and other supernatural creatures are part and parcel of Arab folklore. Consequently, they are feared of, revered and should be appeased. Moreover, the fear of the harmful evil eye, and therefore, the need to protect people and property from its deleterious effects can be reflected in many customs and, in particular, through a large number of expressions, as the following:

māšaḷḷah – (lit. "God willing") is usually used as a sign (often as an interjection), expressing amazement and admiration for a property (a new house, car, etc.) or an action or achievement of a person, mainly a child. The general idea is that this (success, achievement, etc.) is God's wish and may no evil eye harm the person or the object praised.

---

3 The proof that only the word 'dog' and not the whole expression is considered offensive and therefore requires the addition of the parenthesis, is that rarely such a parenthetical expression is used in the case of more offensive expressions, such as *ibn ḥarām* – bastard, *ibn al-qaḥba / aš-šarmūṭa* – son of a whore, and some more.

smallah ʿalēh (lit. "God's name is on him"), i.e. may no evil eye harm him. The expression is often used to express surprise, admiration or praise, only for a human being but not for property.[4]

mxammas (lit. "stopped by the five fingers") is based on the belief that the right palm with clasped fingers aimed at a person can stop his evil eye from harming. Moreover, it is quite common to hear mainly mothers who will use the expression: *xamse* or *xamse fi ʿēno / ʿyūno* – five or five in his eye(s), in reaction to someone who fails to use expressions against the evil eye, while referring to their child, such as those mentioned above.[5]

baraka or *al-baraka* (lit. bless) or *tzīd al-baraka* (lit. "may bless increase") is used in reaction to a statement about e.g., income, winnings, etc.

A few idioms and proverbs, referring to the evil eye, may also be used as possible replies, e.g., *yixzi l-ʿēn ʿannak* – may God drive the evil eye away from you; *ʿēn al-ḥasūd lā tasūd* – may the eye of the envious never prevail, or *ʿēn al-ḥasūd fīha ʿūd* – may the eye of the envious be blinded by a small piece of wood.

Even the pre-Islamic custom of augury (*ʿiyāfa* or *taṭayyur*), i.e. prognostication by the flight of the birds, is echoed in the wish for a safe journey *ʿala ṭ-ṭāʾir al-maymūn* – on the lucky bird.

4. Fatalism

The Arabs strongly believe that anything that happens is in fulfilment of the wish of God, who should be praised for the good and the bad, as succinctly summed up by the dictum *kullo min allāh* – everything is from God. Nevertheless, the fear of death and the wish for long life is throbbing in the heart of all. Hence, there is a large number of expressions that contain the words 'life' or 'living' and some of their derivatives, mainly used as good wishes for long life. E.g., any provider of a service may be thanked by one of the following phrases in addition to the usual phrases for thank you: *allāh yxallīk, allāh yṭawwel ʿumrak, allāh yeḥfaẓak,*

4 See also above p. 32.

5 Artistic drawings showing the open palm are very popular in the Middle East as a protective amulet against the evil eye. They usually can be seen hung in the house, at work, in cars, on necklaces, and on key-rings.

aḷḷāh ydīmak, ʿišt, tʿīš and more, all meaning 'may God give you long life'. Even when a person apologises for forgetting something, saying *ʾāsef, nsīt* – sorry, I forgot, the common reply is *yinsāk al-mōt* – may death forget you. When a person about whom people speak suddenly turns up, he will be greeted with the expression *ʿumrak ṭawīl* – your life is long. Long life is also meant when a person is congratulated for wearing new clothes for the first time with the expressions *tilbasha u-tihrīha* – may you live long enough to wear it and tear it, or *tiqṭaʿha b-ʿaraq al-ʿāfiye* – tear it with your healthy sweat.

Moreover, the commonest expressions for condolences are *fi ḥayātkom* – in your life or *tʿīšū* – may you live long, while a reply to a question such as: *ʿrift al-marḥūm?* – did you know the deceased? is *ʾaywa, yiʿref ḥālo* – yes, may he know himself.

The word *šarr* 'evil' is used in several expressions to wish a person not to be harmed by it. Thus, if a person is, or will be, on a long trip, his parents, wife etc. will announce that *huwwe min ġēr šarr muš hōn* or *mā bikunš hōn* – he – with no bad (reason) – is not or will not be here. Expressions wishing a sick person a speedy recovery are *yibʿid / yiʿfī ʿannak kull šarr* – may God drive all evil away from you, while a person who has just recovered from illness is congratulated with the expressions *rāḥ al-šarr* – evil has gone, or *mā tšūf šarr ʾabadan* – may you never see evil again. An expression used in classical Arabic that has entered the spoken language is *kafāk aḷḷāh šarrahum* – may God protect you against their evil.

5. Friendliness and friendship

Friendliness and friendship are expressed in different ways but mainly by using words:

a. From the semantic field of family when addressing a friend or friends, e.g., *yā ʾaxi* – my brother, *yā ʾuxti* – my sister, *yā ʾixwān* – brothers, *yā xālti* – my maternal aunt (when addressing an older lady); *yā ʿammi* – my paternal uncle (when addressing an older person), *yā ibn ʿammi / yā bint ʿammi* – my cousin;[6] *yā bā* – daddy, *yā mā* – mummy (when addressing an old man or woman); *yā ibni* – my son, *yā binti* – my daughter, when addressing children, *yā bunayya* (from classical Arabic) – my little son, in the diminutive to indicate affection.

6 The last expression is often used by a husband when addressing his wife.

b. Denoting close friendship by using words showing endearment, such as *yā ṣāḥbi, yā ṣadīqi* – my friend, *yā ʿazīzi* – the one who is endeared to me, *yā ḥabībi* – my dear.

c. Employing metaphorically members of the body, such as *yā ʿēni* – my eye, *yā rōḥi* – my soul. The equivalent expressions in Classical Arabic *yā ḥušāšat qalbī* – the last breath of my heart (sic) and *yā filḏat kabidī* – a piece of the flesh of my liver, are rarely used.

d. Denoting the higher position or status of the addressee, e.g., *yā šēx* – oh Sheikh; *yā ʾustāz, yā mʿallim* – oh teacher (for a female *yā mʿallimti*), and *yā ibn ḥalāl – yā bint al-ḥalāl* - the son/daughter of honest people; *yā ḥājj* – oh pilgrim, or simply, *yā sīdi* – Sir!

6. Respect and endearment of the other

These are achieved in various ways, but mainly through showing submissiveness and self-effacing, e.g., *ʿabdak, xaddāmak, ʿabdak al-muxleṣ* – your slave or loyal servant; *huʾmur* – (lit. "give me an order, command me"), *taḥt ʾamrak* – (lit. "I am under your command"), *ʿala rāsi u-ʿēni* – (lit. "on my head and eye"), i.e. at your service, yes, Sir; *bidna riḍākom* – we wish to please you, in many cases used by a son / daughter, showing respect for their parents; *b-xāṭrak / b-xāṭirkum* or *ʿan ʾiznak* – (may I leave) with your permission; *daxīlak* – (lit. "I am your protégé", and therefore under your protection), i.e. do me a favour, or *maḥsūbak* – (lit. "I am under your protection"), i.e. at your service; *bidūn muʾāxaza* (lit. "without holding it against me"), i.e. excuse me; *wa-lā ʿalēk ʾamr, iftaḥ al-bāb* – don't take it as an order, please open the door; *wa-lā tizġar* – (lit. don't feel belittled / humiliated), please do what I ask; *bidūn ġalabe / taklīf / ʾizʿāj* – (lit. "no forcing / imposing / disturbing"), i.e. (sorry) to trouble you.

7. Great concern about the welfare and well-being of the other

This is achieved mainly with the help of words such as *saʿāda* (happiness), *rāḥa* (convenience / comfort), *salāme, ʿāfye* and *ṣaḥḥa* (health) and their derivatives. E.g., *furṣa saʿīda* – (lit. "happy occasion") i.e. nice to have met you, *ʾasʿada llāhu ṣabāḥakom / masāʾakom* – may God make your morning / evening a happy one; *šoftak rāḥa* – it is a pleasure seeing you; *taʿabkom / ġilbitkom rāḥa* – (lit. "your trouble is our pleasure"), used as a reply to *ġallabnākom* – we have troubled you. *salāmtak* – (lit. "your well-being"), i.e. be well, and even 'thanks'!; *aḻḻāh ysallmak* – may God give you health; *maʿa s-salāma* – (lit. "with health"), i.e. bye, bye, bon voyage; *al-ḥamdu li-ḻḻāh ʿala s-salāme* – (lit. "thank God for your health"), used to welcome someone who has returned from a journey, or someone who has recovered from illness; *yesallem ʾīdēk* – (lit. "may God protect your hands"), i.e. mainly 'thank you for the delicious meal'; *aḻḻāh yaʿṭīk al-ʿāfyeh* – (lit. "may God give you health"), i.e. thanks; well done!; *ʿawāfi* or *bi-l-ʿawāfi* – (lit. "with healths" (sic) – bon appétit; *ṣaḥḥ badano* (lit. "may his body be well"), i.e. may he be healthy and well.

A large number of expressions contain the word *xēr* or the plural *xērāt* (good, goodness), implying the goodness of God [compare the expression *xēr aḻḻāh* – (lit. "the goodness of God"), indicating the abundance of good things such as food, wealth, etc., e.g., *qaddamū fi l-ḥafleh xēr aḻḻāh* – they served in the party a variety of delicious food in large quantities]: *ṣabāḥ al-xēr* and *masāʾ al-xēr* – good morning / evening; *tiṣbaḥ ʿala xēr* – (lit. "may you wake up on goodness"), i.e. I wish you a good sleep; good night; *kull ʿām u-intū bi-xēr* – happy New Year; *xēr, ʾinšaḻlah* – (lit. "good things, God willing"), i.e. what happened? *kattar xērak* – (lit. "may God increase your goodness, reward"), i.e. thank you very much.

8. Exaggeration and 'love for the magnitude'

Many expressions may reflect an inclination to exaggerate on the part of the user, who likes to use hyperbole, usually in replies. This tendency is widely used to enhance the utterance or to achieve emphasis, often implying generosity and kindness. This may be gained:

a. By using the dual form:

A *marḥaba!* – hello!
B *marḥabtēn!* – double hello!

A *ʾahlan* (*wa-sahlan*) – welcome!
B *ʾahlēn* (*wa-sahlēn*) – double welcome!

A *ṣaḥḥa* – bon appétit!
B *ṣaḥtēn* – double bon appétit!

b. By using the plural:
ṣabāḥ al-xērāt or *ṣabāḥ al-xērāt u-l-barakāt* – (lit. "morning of many good things and blessings"), i.e. good morning! *salamāt!* (lit. "many peaces"), i.e. hi! hello! *marāḥib* (lit. "many *marḥabas*") – hello; *kīf al-ʾaḥwāl?* – how are things?, alongside *kīf al-ḥāl?* – how are you?

c. By using hundreds, thousands, etc.
E.g., *mīt* / *ʾalf* / *mīt ʾalf marḥaba* – hundred, thousand / hundred thousand hellos; *yā mīt ṣabāḥ* (lit. "hundred mornings"), i.e. good morning!; *ʾalf mabrūk* – (lit. "thousand blessings"), i.e. be blessed for (the new baby, house, car, clothes, degree, etc.); *ʾalf salām* – thousand greetings; *ʾalf šukur* – thousand thanks; *mīt hala fīkom* – hundred welcome; also with the word *marra* (times) the numbers twenty, hundred, thousand, hundred thousand and even million have been recorded, e.g., *ʿišrīn* / *mīt* / *ʾalf* / *mīt ʾalf* / *malyōn marra ṭalabt minnak* – I have begged you 20 ... times.

d. By using a synonym
ṣaḥḥa u-ʿāfye – (lit. "health and well-being"), i.e. bon appétit (the equivalent expression in Classical Arabic *hanīʾan marīʾan* – bon appétit, may also be used); *yā hala* – *yā marḥaba* – welcome!

e. By using two separate words
E.g., *bi-l-hana wa-š-šifa* (lit. "with pleasure and health"), *nhārak saʿīd umbārak* – (lit. "your day is happy and blessed") – good morning.

9. Generosity and kindness
It is one of the famous qualities of the Arab since pre-Islamic times, especially in the context of hospitality and philanthropy. This can be mainly demonstrated by the warm welcome of a guest and all the customs associated with entertaining visitors at home as well as other deeds which may evince the kind nature of the person. Linguistically speaking, the scores of invitation formulae, table etiquette and the exchange of courteous phrases between the host and his guest may also reflect kindness and generosity. E.g., *bēti bētak* – my house is yours; *tfaḍḍal* – (lit. "have the kindness"), i.e. please, and the reply *ʾafḍalt* (I am honoured); *nawwart ad-dunyā ʿalēnā* – (lit. "you have lit the world on us"), i.e. you are very welcome here; *ʿāš man šāfak* – (lit. "seeing you prolongs the life of people"); *al-ʾakl ʿala qadd al-maḥabba* – (lit. "the food measures the love

for you"), we are very happy to see you with us. Other expressions used in different contexts also indicate appreciation for the kindness showed by the individual. E.g., a reply for a compliment is usually *hāda min luṭfak* – (lit. "this is because of your kindness"), i.e. you are kind, while an acknowledgement of a good deed would usually be answered with *ʾastaġfir aḷḷāh* – I am asking forgiveness from God, indicating humility.

10. Humour

Some daily polite expressions may demonstrate humour, sarcasm or irony, yet over the years they have become more "mild". Nevertheless, they may still be amusing, often making the speaker and the hearer laugh. E.g., some of the "alternative" replies to the greeting *ṣabāḥ al-xēr* (good morning) may be *ṣabāḥ al-full / al-yasmīn* – morning of the jasmin, *ṣabāḥ al-ward* – morning of the rose, *ṣabāḥ al-qišṭa* – morning of cream, *ṣabāḥ al-ʿandalīb* – morning of the nightingale. An example for sarcasm, though not meant to be, is the expression *aḷḷāh yaʿṭīk* – God may / will give you, and even *aḷḷāh yaʿṭīnā u-yaʿṭīk* – God may / will give us and you, which are a polite refusal to a beggar.

The most peculiar idiom, however, is no doubt *ḥmātak bitḥubbak* – (lit. "your mother-in-law loves you"), i.e. come and join us at the table, an invitation usually extended to someone who is passing by and wishing eaters 'bon appétit'.

11. Gestures

Some gestures are part of 'body language' and are used by speakers in various situations as polite expressions. For example, polite refusal to have more food as 'a second helping' is expressed by putting the right hand on the heart and saying *lā waḷḷāh* – no, by God, *lā šukran* – no thanks, *bi-l-ʾafrāḥ / bi-faraḥ wlādkom* – on happy occasions / at the wedding of your children, or simply *al-ḥamdu li-ḷḷāh* – praise to God.

An indication, confirming one's readiness to help is demonstrated by pointing at one's eyes and say *min hāy qabl hāy* – (lit. "from this one before that one"), i.e. willingly; also by touching the forehead and then the heart and often kissing the tip of the index finger and the middle finger, saying *ʿala r-rās u-l-ʿēn* or *ʿala rāsi u-ʿēni* – (lit. "on the head and on the eye", or "on my head and my eye"), i.e. I shall be happy to give you what you want.

A gesture indicating the disbelief of a person in what had been said is achieved by touching the upper part of the right cheek close to the eye with the tip of the index finger of the right hand and saying in the interrogative tone *ʿalēna?* (lit. "on us?"), i.e. are you making fun of me? Are you kidding? Do you think I believe you?

12. Language

Although the morphology and syntax of the phrases and expressions are a subject of its own, one phenomenon is worth mentioning. A large number of the phrases are formed according to the pattern of the passive participle, e.g., *mabrūk* – (blessed, good luck), *mamnūn*, *maškūr* – thanks, *mašrūb* – thanks, but no more drinks, *maʾkūl* – thanks but no more food, *maqbūl* – may your prayer, pilgrimage or fast in Ramaḍān be accepted by God, *muwaffaq* – good luck.

Conclusions

The paper has attempted to discuss and illustrate the ways in which language, in our case the Palestinian dialects, is used for politeness, thus indicating tendencies, based on customs and manners, relating to the Arab society and to Arab culture. Some of those may reflect some facets of the mentality of the society.

The daily phrases and expressions used in the region prove a strong belief in God and Islam, loyalty to the family at large, appreciation of friendship and friendliness, readiness to offer services and help, generosity and kindness, and last but not least, self-respect and honouring the other. Moreover, the expressions that Arabs use prove that they aspire to achieve and wish others a long, happy and comfortable life.

On the other hand, the phrases and expressions in the Palestinian dialect may reflect some superstitions current in the society and a strong feeling that all human beings are exposed to the vagaries of fate. What is more, the courtesies used clearly demonstrate practices and characteristics which are unacceptable (but still exist) in many areas in Western society, such as the tendency to fantasise and exaggerate, and the discriminative attitude towards females.

Bibliography

Alcalay, Ben-Zion. 1995. *Berachot, ginunim ve-nimusim ba-'aravit ha-'erets-yisre'elit.* Israel: The Open University (in Hebrew).

Dickson, Harold R. P. 1949. *The Arab of the Desert.* London: Allen & Unwin.

Elihai, Yohanan. 1977. *Milon 'ivri-'aravi la-safa ha-'aravit ha-meduberet.* Jerusalem: Hotsa'at Yanets.

Lane, Edward W. 1986. *An Account of the Manners and Customs of the Modern Egyptians, written in Egypt during the years 1833–1835.* London: Darf Publishers.

Piamenta, Moshe. 1979. *Islam in Everyday Arabic Speech.* Leiden: Brill.

Piamenta, Moshe. 1983. *The Muslim Conception of God and Human Welfare.* Leiden: Brill.

Shivtiel, Avihai. 2004. "Taḳālīd", *The Encyclopaedia of Islam,* 2nd edition, Supplement, 774–779. Leiden: Brill.

Shivtiel, Avihai. 2008. "Politeness", *Encyclopedia of Arabic Language and Linguistics,* vol. III, 658–663. Leiden: Brill.

Formules et dérivés « formulatifs » en arabe

Pierre Larcher, Université de Provence

0. Introduction

Tous les arabisants connaissent des mots (verbes et noms), tels que *(al)-basmala, sabḥala, ḥamdala* etc., dérivés respectivement de *bi-smi-llāh, al-ḥamdu li-llāh, subḥāna llāh*… A ma connaissance, néanmoins, l'inventaire de ces mots reste à faire et, plus encore, la « théorie » de leur formation et de leur interprétation. Certes, ceux des arabisants qui connaissent la grammaire arabe traditionnelle savent que celle-ci en traite sous l'appellation générique de *naḥt*. Ce terme désigne proprement une entaille, et, par métaphore, dans la terminologie linguistique, un procédé de *composition*, par télescopage d'au moins deux mots, e.g. *ṣildim* « aux sabots durs » (< *ṣild* « dur » + *ṣadam* « choc ») *ḥabqarr* « grêlon » (< *ḥabb qarr* « graines de froid »). Le mot formé par *naḥt* (*kalima manḥūta*) n'est pas sans ressembler à l'anglais *stagflation* (< stagnation and inflation) ou *Reaganomics* (< Reagan's economics). Mais, quand le résultat est, comme dans le cas des verbes et des noms qui nous intéressent ici, une forme régulière, c'est tout autant un procédé de *dérivation*, à partir d'une base complexe. De même, ceux des arabisants connaissant la linguistique occidentale moderne sont tentés, dans la mesure où, dans la paraphrase que donnent les grammairiens et lexicographes arabes de cette catégorie particulière de *kalimāt manḥūta*, la base de ces mots apparaît dans le champ de *qāla/qawl* « dire », de les appeler à la suite du linguiste français Emile Benveniste (1902 - 1976) (Benveniste (1958 [1966]), « délocutifs » (e.g. Fleisch, 1968 : 161, 247 n. 21 et 1979 : 329 et n. 21, 439).

1. Inventaire

A ma connaissance, la liste la plus complète de ces mots se trouve dans le *Muzhir* (tome I, p. 483-484) de Suyūṭī (m. 911/1505). Elle représente la compilation des sources suivantes : le *Fiqh al-luġa* de Ibn Fāris, m. 395/ 1004 (le *Muzhir* reproduit l'entièreté du *bāb al-naḥt*, p. 271 de notre édition du *Fiqh al-luġa*) ; le *ʾIṣlāḥ al-manṭiq* de Ibn al-Sikkīt (m. 244/858 ?, p. 303 de notre édition du *ʾIṣlāḥ*) et le *Tahḏīb* qu'en a fait Tibrīzī

(m. 502/1109, p. 650 de notre édition du *Tahḏīb*) [1] ; le *Fiqh al-luġa* de Ṯaʿālibī, m. 429/1038 (le *Muzhir* ne reproduit que partiellement le chapitre que Ṯaʿālibī leur consacre, p. 206-207 de notre édition du *Fiqh al-luġa*) [2] ; le *Ṣiḥāḥ* de Ǧawharī (m. vers 400/1009-10), le *Tanwīr* de Ibn Diḥya (m. 633/1235). Voici la liste qu'on peut en abstraire par ordre alphabétique de l'arabe (avec la base donnée dans les paraphrases) :

1. *basmala* (< *bi-smi llāh* « au nom d'Allah »)
2. *jaʿfada* (ou *jaʿfala*) (< *juʿiltu fidā-k* « je sois fait ta rançon ! »)
3. *ḥasbala* (< *ḥasbiya llāh* « Allah me suffit ! »)
4. *ḥamdala* (< *al-ḥamdu li-llāh* « Louange à Allah ! »)
5. *ḥawqala* (ou *ḥawlaqa*) (< *lā ḥawla wa-lā quwwata ʾillā bi-llāh* « il n'est de puissance et de force qu'en Allah »)
6. *ḥayʿala* (< *ḥayya ʿalā l-ṣalāti, ḥayya ʿalā l-falāḥ* « Venez à la prière, venez au salut ! »)
7. *damʿaza* (< *ʾadāma llāhu ʿizzaka* « Allah fasse durer ta puissance !»)
8. *sabḥala* (< *subḥāna llāh* « Gloire à Allah ! »)
9. *samʿala* (< *salām ʿalaykum* « Salut à vous ! »)
10. *ṭalbaqa* (< *ʾaṭāla llāhu baqāʾaka* « Allah te donne longue vie ! »)
11. *kabtaʿa* (pas de paraphrase, mais < *kabata llāhu l-ʿaduww* (ou *ʿaduwwak* « Allah culbute l'/ton ennemi ») [3]
12. *mašʾala* (ou *maškana* (< *mā šāʾa llāh* (*kān*) « Ce qu'Allah veut (est) »)
13. *haylala* (ou *hallala*) (< *lā ʾilāha ʾillā llāhu* « il n'est de dieu qu'Allah »).

On notera que tous ces mots sont plus souvent cités sous la forme du nom que du verbe, ce qui peut constituer une indication et sur leur formation et sur leur interprétation. Tous sont dérivés de formules et on peut les appeler, pour cette raison, « formulatifs » (Larcher, 1983). Tous ont la forme *faʿlala*, sauf un *hallala* qui a la forme *faʿʿala*. Rappelons qu'une formule se caractérise par deux traits : 1) quelle que soit sa forme (mot, syntagme, proposition, phrase…), elle a un emploi holophrastique; 2) quel que soit son sens littéral, son vrai sens est sa valeur d'emploi,

---

1 Le *Muzhir* cite en fait le *Tahḏīb* et non le *ʾIṣlāḥ*. Le *Tahḏīb* ajoute en effet aux trois exemples du *Iṣlāḥ* trois autres exemples.

2 Ṯaʿālibī indique qu'il reprend al-Farrāʾ (m. 207/822) et autres.

3 La première paraphrase est dans le *Lisān al-ʿArab* de Ibn Manẓūr, m. 711/1311 (art. KBT), la seconde dans le *ʾAsās* de Zamaḫšarī, m. 538/1144 (art. KBT).

qu'il n'est pas toujours facile de déterminer. A ces deux traits s'ajoute le caractère figé de la formule, le figement pouvant intervenir à tout moment. Ainsi, alors que Ṯaʿālibī paraphrase *ḥayʿala* par *ḥikāyat qawl al-muʾaḏḏin ḥayya ʿalā l-ṣalāti, ḥayya ʿalā l-falāḥ*, Ibn Diḥya le paraphrase par *qawl ḥayya ʿalā l-šayʾ* et le fait suivre par *ḥayhala* (< *ḥayyahalā bi-š-šayʾ*) (*Muzhir*, t. I, p. 483). Il vient ainsi rappeler qu'il fut un temps où *ḥayya ʿalā...* était une interjection pouvant se construire avec un objet variable [4]. Par suite l'expression *ḥayʿala* n'était qu'un simple « interjectif » (Larcher, 1983), ce qu'est toujours *ḥayhala*, mais pas encore un « formulatif » [5].

A la liste de Suyūṭī, on pourrait sans doute ajouter, pour la période ancienne, au moins une unité : *baʾbaʾa*. Ce dernier, à côté d'un emploi comme « appellatif » (Larcher, 1983), de sens « dire *bābā* », a aussi un emploi comme formulatif de sens « dire *bi-ʾabī ʾanta* 'Mon père soit ta rançon !' », qui le fait apparaître comme un hyponyme de *jaʿfada* [6]. Et on pourrait ajouter, pour des périodes plus récentes, deux autres unités : *faḏlaka* (< *fa-ḏālika* « ce qui fait... ») et *fanqala*, étudié par Shivtiel (1995) (< *fa-ʾin qultum/qīla..., qulnā...* « si vous dites/on dit..., nous dirons... »). L'article FA<u>DH</u>LAKA de *EI*[2] suggère que le premier vient de l'époque ottomane et Shivtiel (1995) donne le second comme une création même de l'écrivain égyptien Ṭāhā Ḥusayn (1889-1973), qui l'emploie à deux reprises, une fois au singulier et une fois au pluriel, dans sa célèbre autobiographie *al-ʾAyyām* (t. 2, p. 158 et p. 160). Si cela est, cela veut dire que ce procédé de formation, que nous allons maintenant étudier, continue d'avoir une certaine productivité.

---

4 *Lisān al-ʿArab* (art. ḤYY) donne ainsi *ḥayya ʿalā l-ṯarīd, al-ġadāʾ, al-ḫayr...*

5 C'est sûrement le *ḥayhala* « interjectif », et non « formulatif », qu'on trouve dans le vers cité par Ibn Fāris d'après al-Ḫalīl (*Fiqh al-luġa*, p. 271 repris dans le *Muzhir*, t. 1, p. 482) *ʾaqūlu lahā wa-damʿu l-ʿayni jārin / ʾa-lam tuḥzinki ḥayhalatu l-munādī* « Je lui dis, tandis que coulent les larmes de l'œil / 'N'est-ce pas le Hé ! Ho ! de l'appelant qui t'a attristée ?' ».

6 Les deux sens sont dans le *Lisān al-ʿArab* (art. BʾBʾ). Ce dictionnaire signale bien le caractère bipolaire de l'appellatif (comme aujourd'hui encore en Orient, non seulement le fils peut dire à son père, mais encore le père à son fils *bābā*). Pour le formulatif, il donne pour *bi-ʾabī ʾanta* la paraphrase *ʾafdī-ka bi-ʾabī* « je te fais rançon de mon père ».

2. Formation

Il ne suffit pas de dire que ces mots ont pour base une formule, dont ils sont dérivés. Encore convient-il de se demander comment ils sont formés, à partir de cette base. De telles formations montrent bien les limites du principe racine/schème (*root/pattern*), si cher aux arabisants occidentaux. Certes, le mot, comme tout mot régulier de l'arabe, est analysable en un ensemble de consonnes d'une part, un schème (structure syllabique + voyelles) d'autre part. Il est cependant clair que dans *basmala*, ce n'est pas le quadruplet BSML à lui seul qui représente la base *bismillāh*, c'est tout autant la structure syllabique du dérivé : *bas-mal*, en corrélation avec celle de la base *bis-mil-lāh*. Et c'est évidemment cette correspondance formelle qui permet aussitôt de reconnaître la base dans le dérivé. Autrement dit, la signification lexicale (attachée au radical dans les langues indo-européennes et à la racine consonantique dans les langues sémitiques, par opposition à la signification grammaticale, attachée aux affixes dans les langues indo-européennes, au schème dans les langues sémitiques) déborde ici sur le schème lui-même. Et, par suite encore, on ne voit pas bien quelle signification grammaticale aurait le schème…

Mais la théorie arabe du *naḥt* est aussi prise en défaut. Pour plusieurs de ces formules, le dérivé se présente sous la forme de deux variantes. C'est d'abord le cas de *jaʿfada/jaʿfala*. *Jaʿfada* est donné par Tibrīzī, selon *Muzhir* (t. I, p. 483), mais notre édition du *Tahḏīb* (p. 650) donne *jaʿfala*. Ibn Diḥya dans le *Tanwīr*, selon *Muzhir* (t. I, p. 484), donne *jaʿfada*, en indiquant que « *jaʿfala* avec *lām* est une faute » (*wa-l-jaʿfala bi-l-lām ḫaṭaʾ*). Mais qualifier cette variante de faute est une démarche prescriptive, qui a le mérite, sur le plan descriptif, d'en présupposer l'existence. La première variante suit le processus décrit pour le *naḥt* par Ibn Mālik (m. 672/1274) dans le *Tashīl* (cité dans *Muzhir*, I, p. 485, soit p. 262 de notre édition du *Tashīl*), à propos d'une autre catégorie de *faʿlala*, celle servant de base à la formation d'un adjectif de relation correspondant à un syntagme (e.g. *Imruʾ al-Qays* > *marqasī* « relatif à Imruʾ al-Qays ») :

« on forme à partir des deux éléments du composé un *faʿlala*, avec la première et la deuxième radicales de chacun des deux : si la deuxième radicale du second élément est faible, la forme est complétée avec la troisième radicale ou celle du premier élément, puis on forme l'adjectif de relation » (*qad yubnā min juzʾay al-murakkab faʿlala bi-fāʾ kull minhumā wa-ʿaynihi fa-ʾin iʿtallat ʿayn al-ṯānī kamula al-bināʾ bi-lāmihī ʾaw bi-lām al-ʾawwal wa-nusiba ʾilayhi*).

Un exemple comme *ḥay'ala* (< **ḥa**y**y**a 'a**l**ā l-ṣalāti, **ḥa**y**y**a 'a**l**ā l-falāḥ) suit également cette règle, mais non la seconde variante *ja'fala* : elle prend les deux premières radicales du premier mot, puis la première radicale du second et, enfin, ce *lām* qu'Ibn Diḥya juge fautif. Certes, il peut sembler l'être avec la paraphrase du nom *al-ja'fala* que donne notre édition du *Tahḏīb* de Tibrīzī (p. 650) : *qawl ju'iltu fidāk* [7]. Mais il ne l'est plus avec celle donnée du verbe *ja'fala* par le *Šarḥ al-Tashīl* de Ibn Mālik (t. III, p. 449) : *qāla ja'ala-nī llāhu fidā'a-ka* « Allah me fasse ta rançon ! ». Cette dernière paraphrase suggère que le *lām* de *ja'fala* n'est plus celui du verbe *ja'ala* mais celui du nom *Allāh* et qu'il doit sa place, qui ne respecte pas ici l'ordre des éléments de la formule, à une attraction paradigmatique, celle des formules où l'élément *Allāh* figure en dernière position : Ibn Mālik cite *ja'fala*, comme dernier exemple d'une série de cinq, dont les quatre premiers sont *basmala*, *ḥasbala*, *sabḥala* et *ḥamdala*.

Plusieurs exemples, *ḥamdala* (< al-**ḥamdu li-llāh**), *ḥasbala* (<**ḥasb**iya **llāh**), *sabḥala* (< **subḥ**āna **llāh**), prennent les trois radicales du premier mot, toutes « saines », et la première du second. Mais *kabta'a* < **kab**a**t**a llāhu l-'aduww (ou 'aduwwak) prend les trois radicales du verbe et la première radicale de l'objet, *sam'ala* (< **s**alā**m** '**a**laykum) prend les 1ère et 3ème radicales du nom et les 1ère et 2ème radicales de *'alā*, *dam'aza* et *ṭalbaqa* les 1ère et 3ème radicales des verbes et la 1ère et 2ème radicales des noms. Ces deux dernières formations ont un double intérêt : non seulement, elles montrent qu'elles ne se règlent pas sur la racine consonantique des éléments, mais sur les consonnes effectivement prononcées, mais encore que leur base véritable est ***ṭāla baqā'uka*** et ***dāma*** *'izzuka*, les phrases *'aṭāla llāhu baqā'aka* et *'adāma llāhu 'izzaka* représentant l'islamisation de formules antérieures à l'islam [8].

7 C'est certainement ce qui explique l'existence d'une troisième variante que l'on trouve dans le *Fiqh al-luġa* (p. 207, passage non repris par *Muzhir*) de Ṯa'ālibī : *al-ja'lafa*, paraphrasé par *ḥikāyat qawl ju'iltu fidā'a-ka*. Mais l'éditeur du *Fiqh al-luġa* ajoute en note : *fī riwāya al-ja'fala wa-huwa taṣḥīf bi-ma'nā-hu* « dans une version, *al-ja'lafa*, mais c'est une erreur de lecture, avec ce sens ». On soupçonne donc que c'est l'éditeur qui, compte tenu de la paraphrase, a remis le *lām* à sa place…

8 Elles s'adressent à un souverain, cf. *Alf layla wa-layla*, III, 79 'Abū Qīr wa-'Abū Ṣīr, *wa-qabbala 'Abū Ṣīr yad al-malik wa-da'ā lahu bi-dawām al-'izz wa-ṭūl al-baqā'* « 'Abū Ṣīr baisa la main du roi et implora pour lui puissance qui dure et longue vie ». Ġazālī (*'ayyuhā l-walad*, p. 49) la censure en ces termes : *wa-man da'ā li-ṭūl baqā'ihim fa-qad 'aḥabba 'an yu'ṣā llāhu fī l-'arḍ* « qui implore longue vie pour eux [i.e. émirs et sultans], c'est qu'il a voulu qu'on désobéisse à Dieu sur terre ».

En fait, il n'y a pas de règle. Ou, plus exactement, il n'y a pas d'autre règle que pragmatique : faire en sorte que la base soit aussitôt reconnue dans le dérivé. C'est ce que montre l'examen des deux variantes *maš'ala* et *maškana*. Les éditeurs du *Muzhir* substituent *maš'ala* à *maškana*, en notant (*Muzhir*, t. I, p. 484, n. 1) : « dans l'original, il y a *maškana*, mais nous sommes d'avis que c'est *maš'ala* » (*wa-fī al-'aṣl* maškana *wa-narā 'annahā* maš'ala). Cette substitution s'explique par la paraphrase donnée par le *Muzhir* : *qawl mā šā'a llāh*, qui n'explique pas le *n*. Inversement, l'auteur de l'article Compounds de *EALL* (I, p. 453) cite *maškana*, en indiquant qu'il vient de *mā šā'a llāh kān* « Whatever God intends, will happen ». Au passage est ainsi rappelé que la formule *mā šā'a llāh* est en fait la troncation de la phrase *mā šā'a llāh kān*, phrase positive éventuellement citée avec sa contrepartie négative : *wa-mā lām yaša' lam yakun* (« et ce qu'il ne veut pas, n'existe pas »). Si c'est la troncation de la phrase entière qui fait du segment *mā šā'a llāh* une formule d'exclamation admirative, la phrase entière vient rappeler la conception islamique des choses : l'objet admiré n'existe que par la volonté divine…

Le même pragmatisme se retrouve avec les deux variantes *ḥawlaqa* et *ḥawqala*, données par Tibrīzī (*Tahḏīb*, p. 650). Ibn Diḥya proscrit la seconde : « ne dis pas : *ḥawqala*, en mettant le *qāf* avant » (*wa-lā taqul* ḥawqala *bi-taqdīm al-qāf*), mais cette fois-ci avec un bon argument : «car *al-ḥawlaqa* est la démarche du vieillard chétif » (*fa-'inna* l-ḥawqala *mišyat al-šayḫ al-ḍa'īf*) (*Muzhir*, t. 1, p. 483-484).

3. De la formation à l'interprétation

Pour les grammairiens arabes, le *naḥt* est un « genre d'abréviation » (*jins min al-iḫtiṣār*), cf. Ibn Fāris, *Fiqh al-luġa* (p. 271), repris dans *Muzhir* (I, p. 482). C'est pourquoi on retrouve quelques-uns des *fa'lala* ici cités dans l'article Abbreviations de *EALL* (I, p. 1-5). L'auteur les range dans la sous-catégorie des « contractions », servant à former un « portmanteau word » [9]. L'auteur rappelle qu'il s'agit du *naḥt* en renvoyant à l'article « Compounds ». Mais il ajoute : « To all intents and purposes, the word *naḥt* corresponds to an acronym, i.e. a word formed from the abbreviation of, in most cases, the initial letters of each word in the construct », donnant pour exemples *basmala*, *ḥamdala* et *ṣalwala* (< *ṣallā llāh 'alayhi*).

9 En français nous parlons de mot-valise (sens de l'anglais portmanteau), mais parlons cependant de morphème « porte-manteau » pour le morphème ayant plus d'un signifié.

Même si ces formations partagent avec les acronymes de constituer de nouveaux mots, aucune d'elles cependant n'est constituée à partir des lettres initiales des mots de la formule de base, mais plutôt de mots ou de parties de mots de cette formule, en respectant, autant que faire se peut, la structure syllabique, voire le vocalisme. Sous ce rapport, on ne dira pas que *ṣalwala* (exemple que je ne connais pas) est dérivé de *ṣallā llāh ʿalayhi*, mais plutôt de **ṣal**lā llāhu ʿalayhi **wa**-sal**la**m, *ṣal-* représentant la première syllabe de *ṣallā*, *wa-* la coordination et *la*, le *la* de *sallama* [10]. L'article « Compounds » de *EALL* (t. I, p. 453) est descriptivement plus adéquat, qui parle seulement de « Acronym-like constructions based on conventional religious expressions or formulae consisting on several elements usually not fully represented in the *naḥt*-construction ». Rappelons que l'arabe possède de véritables acronymes, effectivement obtenus à partir des *lettres* initiales des mots de l'expression complexe qu'ils abrègent, e.g. *ḥamās* (***ḥ****arakat al-***m***uqāwama al-***ʾi***slāmiyya* « mouvement de la résistance islamique »), *ʾamal* (*ʾafwāj al-***m***uqāwama al-***l***ubnāniyya* « détachements de la résistance libanaise »), *fatḥ* (***ḥ****arakat* **t***aḥrīr* ***f****ilasṭīn* « mouvement de libération de la Palestine »). Ils ont la particularité d'être en même temps les homonymes de mots de la langue (« zèle », « espoir », « conquête »), relevant ainsi en même temps du jeu de mots et du double sens : dans le cas de *fatḥ*, l'acronyme est inversé, car dans le « bon » sens (*ḥatf*), il aurait un « mauvais » sens («mort, trépas ») ! (Sur les acronymes, cf., en dernier lieu, Edzard, 2007).

4. Interprétation

4.1. Abréviation : emploi et mention

Mais il y a plus. L'auteur de l'article « Abbreviations » ajoute aux trois exemples précités ceux de *ṭalbaqa* (*ṭāla* [sic] *llāh baqāʾa-hu*), *ḥawqala* ou *ḥawlaqa* (*lā ḥawla wa-lā quwwata ʾillā bi-llāh*), *ṣalʿama* « a synonym of *ṣalwala* », *ḥasbala* (*ḥasbunā allāh*), *mašʾala* (*mā šāʾa llāh*), *sabḥala* (*subḥāna llāh*) et *ḥayʿala* (*ḥayya ʿalā ṣ-ṣalāt*). L'idée d'un *ṣalʿama* comme synonyme de *ṣalwala* ne laisse pas d'étonner ! En fait, on connaît صلعم comme abréviation graphique de *ṣallā llāhu wa-sallama* : graphique, parce qu'elle dispense d'écrire la phrase entière *ṣallā llāhu wa-sallama*, mais non, quand on la lit, de dire la phrase qu'elle abrège. Sous ce rapport صلعم ressemble

10 Compte tenu de ce qui a été dit ci-dessus du *lām* de *jaʿfala*, on pourrait aussi faire l'hypothèse que la base de *ṣalwala* est en fait l'une des variantes nominales de la formule : *ṣalawātu llāhi ʿalayhi (wa-salāmu-hu)*.

à *etc.*. Tout en écrivant les trois lettres e-t-c, on n'en prononce pas moins les deux mots *et cetera*. Je ne sais pas si *ṣalʿama* existe. Mais ce que je sais, c'est que s'il existe, il sera aussitôt interprété (un dérivé faisant toujours référence, sémantiquement, à la façon dont s'emploie sa base), en tant que verbe, comme « écrire (l'abréviation) صلعم » et, en tant que nom, comme « l'abréviation صلعم ». Je ne sais pas non plus si *ṣalwala* existe. Mais ce que je sais, c'est que, s'il existe, il sera aussitôt interprété, en tant que verbe, comme « dire *ṣallā llāhu wa-sallama* » et, en tant que nom, comme « la formule *sallā llāhu wa-sallama* ». Autrement dit, l'auteur de l'article commet une confusion grossière, du point de vue logique, entre *emploi* et *mention* de la formule : صلعم abrège l'emploi de la formule *ṣallā llāhu wa-sallama*, en ce sens que la phrase entière et son abréviation ont exactement la même distribution. Si un pieux musulman prononce le nom de Mahomet (ou l'une de ses qualifications, i.e. *al-nabī, rasūlu llāh*), il le fera aussitôt suivre de l'eulogie *ṣallā llāhu ʿalayhi wa-sallama* (ou variantes). Si maintenant notre pieux musulman écrit le nom de Mahomet, il écrira à sa suite soit l'eulogie, soit son abréviation. En revanche *ṣalwala* abrège la mention de la formule, car il aurait la même distribution, non pas que la formule, mais que son *autonyme*, comme on peut le vérifier au travers des exemples de *basmala* et *bi-smi-llāhi al-raḥmān al-raḥīm*, dans les *Šurūḥ al-Talḫīs*. L'un des commentateurs, en l'espèce Dasūqī (m. 1230/1815), dans le commentaire qu'il fait du *Muḫtaṣar* de Taftazānī, m. 791/1389 (lui-même abrégé du *Talḫīṣ* de Qazwīnī, m. 739/1338) écrit successivement (t. I, p. 6) : *qawlu-hu bi-smi-llāhi r-raḥmān ar-raḥīm fī quwwat qawlinā lā ʾabtadiʾu ʾillā bi-smi-llāh taʿāla li-ʾannahu al-raḥmān al-raḥīm* (« Quand il dit « au nom d'Allah, le Clément, le Miséricordieux », c'est potentiellement comme quand nous disons « Je ne commence qu'au nom d'Allah, le Très-Haut, parce qu'il est le Clément, le Miséricordieux » » et *al-ġaraḍ al-ʾaṣlī min al-basmala al-tabarruk wa-l-istiʿāna bi-smihi taʿāla* « L'objet fondamental de la formule *bi-smi-llāh* est d'obtenir la grâce et de demander l'aide de son nom ». Au passage, on a une description de la valeur pragmatique de cette formule, qui est une formule propitiatoire, qu'on prononce au début d'une entreprise. On le voit : ce qui a la même distribution, ce n'est pas *bi-smi-llāhi* et *basmala*, mais *qawl bismillāhi* et *al-basmala*. Les textes confirment ainsi la paraphrase donnée par les grammairiens cités dans notre texte de référence. Partout apparaît le verbe *qāla* pour le verbe *faʿlala* et le nom *qawl* pour le nom associé *al-faʿlala*. L'adjonction de *ḥikāya* (« citation ») devant *qawl* que fait Ṯaʿālibī dans le *Fiqh al-luġa* (p. 206-207), et non reprise par le *Muzhir*, a en fait pour but de lever l'ambiguïté de *qawl* (qui est celle de tous les *maṣdar*-s), en sélectionnant son sens résultatif (« ce qui est dit »), par opposition à son sens actif (« acte de dire ») : on cite ce qui est dit, non l'acte de dire qui peut seulement être raconté. Le titre complet du chapitre 20 (*fī l-ʾaṣwāt wa-ḥikāyātuhā*) et de la section 7 de ce chapitre (*fī ḥikāyāt ʾaqwāl mutādawila ʿalā l-ʾalsina*) vient toutefois rappeler que Ṯaʿālibī conçoit les « formulatifs » comme un sous-ensemble d'un ensemble plus vaste, celui des expressions linguistiques ayant, à un titre ou un autre, une dimension mimétique (onomatopées, « interjectifs » etc…).

Parmi les paraphrases, on relèvera plus particulièrement celle de Ibn al-Sikkīt, reprise par Tibrīzī, où le nom *al-faʿlala* et sa paraphrase en *qawl X* sont systématiquement dans le champ de *ʾakṯara min*…. Alors que *ʾakṯara al-qawl* signifie plutôt « dire beaucoup », *ʾakṯara min qawl*… signifie nettement « dire trop ». Un tel contexte ne peut être un hasard : il vient rappeler que ce qui fait la formule, c'est aussi la fréquence d'emploi et que c'est l'emploi fréquent, voire excessif, qui fait le dérivé.

4.2. Un contre-exemple ?

A la p. 484 du t. I du *Muzhir*, on lit cependant (ce qui paraît être toujours une citation du *Tanwīr* de Ibn Diḥya) : « *al-damʿaza* : *ʾadāma llāhu ʿizzaka*. En relève ce que dit le poète : *lā zilta fī saʿdin yadūmu wa-damʿazah*, c'est-à-dire *dawām ʿizz* ». Autrement dit, l'auteur cité n'a pas interprété ici *damʿaza* comme « la formule *ʾadāma llāhu ʿizzaka* », mais comme la synthémisation du syntagme [11] *dawām ʿizz*. La raison tient probablement au fait que *damʿaza* est coordonné ici à une structure *mawṣūf/ṣifa saʿd yadūmu*, avec laquelle *damʿaza* constitue un chiasme :

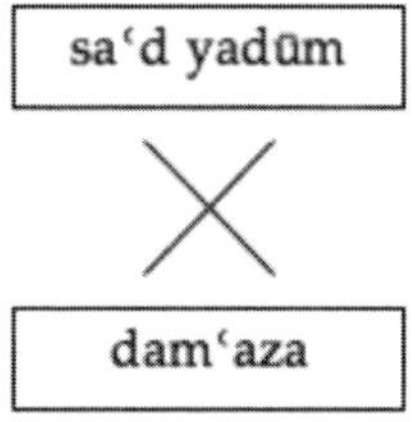

11 Syntagme et synthème sont la terminologie de Martinet (1972[1960]).

Ils se trouvent dans le champ de la préposition *fī* et constituent avec elle un complément prépositionnel du verbe *zilta*. Or celui-ci est lui-même dans le champ de la négation *lā*, ce qui indique que la phrase a elle-même une valeur optative, soit : « puisses-tu être toujours dans un bonheur qui dure et une durable puissance ! » (fr. heur < lat *augurium*). On peut néanmoins se demander si le poète ne souhaite pas à celui auquel il s'adresse à la fois d'être dans un bonheur durable et de recevoir, de la part des autres, de tels souhaits, soit : « Puisses-tu être toujours dans un bonheur qui dure et l'objet de « Que dure ta puissance ! ».

4.3. *Haylala* et *hallala*

Une dernière variante est intéressante. C'est celle de *haylala* et *hallala*. Les deux verbes sont incontestablement formés, par *naḥt*, à partir de *lā ʾilāha ʾillā llāh*, retenant la double allitération en *h* et *l* de la formule. Le fait cependant que tous les deux commencent par *h* et que dans le premier des deux ce *h* soit suivi de *y* suggère que la base de la formation est le segment (lā ʾilā)**ha ʾillā llāh** (le *y* représentant la *hamza*). Par suite, le second pourrait être compris comme un simple doublet du premier, par assimilation de ce *y* à *l* (*haylala* > *hallala*) : on sait que les formes I quadrilitère et II trilitère se superposent morphologiquement, quant à la structure syllabique et au vocalisme, ne différant que par le fait que les 2ème et 2ème radicales sont différentes dans la I quadrilitère, mais identiques dans le II trilitère :

$$R_1aR_2R_3aR_4a$$
$$R_1aR_2R_2aR_3a$$

Il est pourtant facile de montrer que, sur le plan sémantique, *hallala* ne constitue pas un simple doublet de *haylala*, mais, au contraire, un véritable dédoublement. Récemment, lisant avec mes étudiants la *Sīrat Baybarṣ*, dans la version damascène, publié par l'IFEAD, nous avons trouvé cette phrase (t. II, p. 30) :

وقبض على اتنين طالعين من تهليله

wa-qabaḍ ʿalā ətnēn ṭālʿīn min tahlīle [12]

« il se saisit de deux [hommes] sortant d'une tahlîlé »

12 Je dois à Katia Zakharia, cooéditrice de la *sīra*, cette lecture.

Il est clair que *tahlīle* ne désigne pas ici la formule *lā ʾilāha ʾillā llāh,* mais, comme *maṣdar al-marra,* UNE séance de *tahlīl,* c'est-à-dire une réunion (sauf erreur de type mystique) où se trouve répétée cette formule. Le verbe *hallala* se trouve ainsi à l'intersection des deux types de « formulatifs » de l'arabe :

1) d'une part ceux formés par contraction de la formule dans un schème *faʿlala.* Le verbe *faʿlala* (s'il existe) ne signifie rien d'autre que prononcer cette formule et le nom associé désigne la formule elle-même
2) d'autre part ceux formés par dérivation à partir de l'élément essentiel de la formule, généralement un nom, et donnant un verbe *faʿʿala.* Le verbe ne signifie pas simplement « dire X », mais plus exactement « faire ce que l'on fait quand on dit X ». On a ainsi à côté de *sabḥala* le verbe *sabbaḥa* « glorifier (Allah) », de *ḥamdala, ḥammada* « louanger (Allah) », de *jaʿfadaljaʿfala, faddā-hu* « témoigner à quelqu'un un dévouement sans bornes » …[13]

Que *faʿlala* renvoie aux mots eux-mêmes, par opposition à *faʿʿala* qui renvoie à la valeur pragmatique de leur énonciation, est bien attesté par le fait que quand on n'a pas de *faʿʿala* à côté de *faʿlala,* il faut alors recourir à une périphrase comme dans l'exemple tiré du conte de ʾAbū Qīr et ʾAbū Ṣīr (cf. *supra,* n. 8).

4.4. *fadlaka* et *fanqala*

Les deux formations plus récentes que sont *faḏlaka* et *fanqala* sont également intéressantes. Si, par leur forme, elles relèvent de *faʿlala,* par leur sens, elles sont plus proches de *hallala* et donc de *faʿʿala.*

Le verbe *faḏlaka* ne signifie certainement pas, en effet, « dire *fa-ḏālika* », ni le nom *al-faḏlaka* « la formule *fa-ḏālika* ». En fait, *faḏlaka* désigne bien l'opération dont les mots *fa-ḏālika* (« ce qui fait… ») sont le signe, à savoir une addition ou somme aboutissant à un résultat ou total. Et c'est en ce sens qu'on le trouve dans le *Minhāj* d'al-Maḫzūmī (époque fatimide-ayyoubide, soit VI/XIIe siècle), selon Cahen (1962 [1977]), qui précise même en note (p. 272 [50], n. 2) que « Les totaux intermédiaires sont souvent introduits (Makhzūmī et papyrus) par *fadhalika,* et par

13 Les deux premiers verbes sont, par exemple, dans le *Šarḥ al-Tashīl* de Ibn Mālik (III, p. 451) avec les paraphrases respectives *qāla subḥāna llāh* et *al-ḥamdu li-llāh,* le troisième dans le *Lisān al-ʿArab* (art. FDY) avec la paraphrase *qāla juʿiltu fidāk.* D'une manière générale, grammairiens et lexicographes arabes ne distinguent pas les deux séries sur le plan sémantique.

conséquence s'appellent *fadhlaka* » (nous conservons la transcription de l'auteur) [14]. Et c'est par métaphore que le terme désigne ensuite une « synthèse », un « résumé », sens qu'il a dans le titre d'ouvrages de l'époque ottomane.

De même, le nom (à défaut du verbe) *fanqala* ne signifie certainement pas « la formule *fa-ʾin qultum/qīla…qulnā…* ». Shivtiel (1995) rejette cependant les traductions de *fanāqil* et *fanqala* par *conventional studies* et *dialectical skill* dans la version anglaise d'*al-ʾAyyām* [15] et suggère que conviendraient mieux *trifles* (fr. « futilités »), *quibbling* (fr. « argutie ») et *sophism*. En fait, il n'y a pas de contradiction. La *fanqala* désigne bien le procédé, éminemment dialectique, par questions et réponses qu'on trouve dans les traités médiévaux : la question (ou plus largement le problème) est introduit par la protase *fa-ʾin qultum/qīla* (on trouve aussi *qulta* et *qāla qāʾilun*) et la réponse par l'apodose *qulnā* (on trouve aussi *qultu*). Et c'est dans ce sens que Baalbaki (1995 : 132) utilise le terme, en le paraphrasant par « hypothetical questions and answers », pour désigner la première des manifestations de la logique dans les ouvrages de grammaire à partir de Mubarrad (m. 285/898) [16]. Mais il est clair que dans le contexte d'*al-ʾAyyām*, très critique à l'égard de l'enseignement d'al-Azhar, le procédé devient le symbole même d'une scolastique figée et synonyme de « vaines arguties » : on n'a fait que glisser de la dénotation objective à la connotation péjorative.

---

14 Compte tenu de cet emploi, la paraphrase la plus exacte de *fa\ḏlaka* serait : « faire ce que l'on fait quand on écrit *fa-ḏālika* ». Les philologues arabes ne sont pas inconscients de la dimension écrite. *Lisān al-ʿArab* paraphrase ainsi *basmala* (art. BSML), à la suite du *Tahḏīb* d'al-Azharī (m. 370/980), par *kataba bi-smi llāh* « écrire *bi-smi llāh* ».

15 On notera que le traducteur français (qui est pourtant, pour la seconde partie, le grand arabisant Gaston Wiet (1887-1971)) se contente de transcrire par deux fois le mot sous la forme *fankala* (p. 242 et p. 243)…

16 Baalbaki, malheureusement, ne référence pas le terme, l'employant comme un terme parfaitement connu en ce sens. On peut penser qu'il l'empoie en fait soit par allusion littéraire à *al-ʾAyyām* (l'étude de Shivtiel date de la même année), soit par référence implicite à Stetkevych (1970 :50) qui donne *fanqala* comme « a frequently used *manḥūt* verb ». Shivtiel (1995) note que « If Stetkevych is right in saying that *fanqalah* is 'frequently used', it is very surprising that no dictionary has recorded the word».

5. Conclusion

Hallala rétablit une continuité entre les deux séries de « formulatifs ». Par sa formation, il relève de la première série, mais, par son sens, de la seconde : *tahlīl* ne désigne pas la formule, mais l'activité au centre de laquelle se trouve l'énonciation de cette formule, c'est-à-dire une espèce de récollection. Si l'on emploie la terminologie benvenistienne de « délocutif », on distinguera alors entre délocutivité morphologique et délocutivité sémantique. Les *fa ʿlala* sont morphologiquement délocutifs, puisque formés sur la « locution », mais sémantiquement des dénominatifs autonymiques, selon l'interprétation que fait Rey-Debove (1975) des délocutifs benvenistiens : rappelons que l'autonyme d'une expression linguistique, quelle que soit la catégorie de cette expression, est toujours un nom. Inversement les *fa ʿʿala* sont morphologiquement des dénominatifs, puisque dérivés d'un nom, sur la racine consonantique desquels ils sont formés, mais sémantiquement délocutifs, en ce qu'ils renvoient à l'emploi de ce nom dans la formule « ...N... ! », soit :

	morphologie	sémantique
fa ʿlala	délocutif	dénominatif autonymique
fa ʿʿala	dénominatif	délocutif

Si l'on veut conserver l'appellation de délocutifs, dans les deux cas, on peut alors distinguer entre les deux séries de « formulatifs » en utilisant la terminologie des *speech acts* de John Langshaw Austin (1911-1960) (Austin 1962[1970]). La première série dénote une activité simplement « locutionnaire » (the locutionary act is the act of saying something), mais la seconde série une activité proprement illocutionnaire (the illocutionary act is the act performed in saying something). On appellera donc les formulatifs de la première série des délocutifs « locutionnaires » (ou « locutoires »), ceux de la seconde série des délocutifs « illocutionnaires » (ou « illocutoires ») (Larcher, 1985).

Références bibliographiques

1. Sources primaires

Alf layla wa-layla, 3 vols. Beyrouth : Dār al-Hilāl. 1958.

Ġazālī (al-). *Lettre au disciple (Ayyuha 'l-walad)*. Traduction française par Toufic Sabbagh. Introduction par George H. Scherer. Troisième édition. Beyrouth : Commission Libanaise pour la traduction des chefs-d'œuvre. 1969.

Ḥusayn, Ṭāhā. *al-ʾAyyām*, t. II, Dār al-Ma ʿārif bi-Miṣr. 1964.

Ibn Fāris, *Ṣāḥibī* = ʾAbū l-Ḥusayn Aḥmad Ibn Fāris *al-Ṣāḥibī fī fiqh al-luġa wa-sunan al-ʿarab fī kalāmihā*, éd. Moustafa El-Chouémi, Coll. Bibliotheca philologica arabica, publiée sous la direction de R. Blachère et J. Abdel-Nour, vol. 1. Beyrouth : A. Badran & Co. 1383/1964.

Ibn Mālik,*Tashīl* = Jamāl al-dīn Muḥammad b. ʿAbd Allāh al-Ṭāʾī al-Jayyānī al-ʾAndalusī, *Tashīl al-fawāʾid wa-takmīl al-maqāṣid*, éd. Muḥammad Kāmil Barakāt, Le Caire, Dār al-Kātib al-ʿarabī li-l-ṭibāʿa wa-l-našr. 1387/1967.

– *Šarḥ al-Tashīl*, éd. ʿAbd al-Raḥmān al-Sayyid et Muḥammad al-Maḫtūn, 4 parties en 2 vols, Le Caire, Hajr. 1410/1990.

Ibn Manẓūr, *Lisān al-ʿArab* = Muḥammad b. Mukarram b. ʿAlī b. ʾAḥmad al-ʾAnṣārī al-ʾIfrīqī al-Miṣrī Jamāl al-dīn ʾAbū l-Faḍl Ibn Manẓūr. *Lisān al-ʿArab al-muḥīṭ*. Ed. par Yūsuf Ḫayyāṭ, 4 vols. Beyrouth : Dār Lisān al-ʿArab. S.d.

Ibn al-Sikkīt, *ʾIṣlāḥ al-manṭiq*, éd. Aḥmad Muḥammad Šākir et ʿAbd al-Sallām Hārūn, Le Caire, Dār al-Maʿārif, 1375/1956.

Sīrat al-Malik al-Ẓāhir Baybarṣ ḥasab al-riwāya al-šāmiyya, éd. G. Bohas et K. Zakharia, t. II, Damas, Institut Français d'Etudes Arabes de Damas, 2001.

Šurūḥ al-Talḫīṣ, 4 vols, Le Caire, Maṭbaʿat ʿĪsā al-Bābī al-Ḥalabī, 1937.

Suyūṭī, *Muzhir* = ʿAbd al-Raḥmān Jalāl al-dīn al-Suyūṭī *al-Muzhir fī ʿulūm al-luġa wa-ʾanwiʿihā*, éd. Muḥammad Aḥmad Jār al-Mawlā, ʿAlī Muḥammad al-Bajāwī et Muḥammad ʾAbū l-Faḍl Ibrāhīm, 2 vols. Le Caire : ʿĪsā al-Bābī al-Ḥalabī. S.d.

Ṯaʿālibī, *Fiqh al-luġa* = ʾAbū Manṣūr Ismāʿīl al-Ṯaʿālibī al-Nīsābūrī, *Kitāb Fiqh al-luġa wa-sirr al-ʿarabiyya*, Beyrouth, Dār al-kutub al-ʿilmiyya, s.d.

Tibrīzī (al-), *Tahḏīb* = al-Ḫaṭīb al-Tibrīzī, *Tahḏīb ʾIṣlāḥ al-manṭiq*, éd. Faḫr al-dīn Qabāwa, Beyrouth, Manšūrāt Dār al-Afāq al-jadīda, 1983.

Zamaḫšarī, *ʾAsās* = ʾAbū l-Qāsim Maḥmūd b. ʿUmar al-Zamaḫšarī, *ʾAsās al-balāġa*, éd. par ʿAbd al-Raḥīm Maḥmūd. Beyrouth : Dār al-maʿrifa. 1399/1979.

2. Sources secondaires

Austin, John Langshaw. 1962. *How to Do Things with Words*. London : Oxford University Press. [Trad. française, *Quand dire, c'est faire*. Paris: Le Seuil, 1970.]

Abdul Sahib Mehdi Ali (2006). « Compounds », *EALL*, vol. I A-Ed, p. 451-455.

Baalbaki, Ramzi. 1995. « The Book in the Grammatical Tradition: Development in Content and Methods », dans George N. Atiyeh (éd.) *The Book in the Islamic World: the written word and communication in the Middle East*, p. 123-139. Albany: State University of New York Press.

Benveniste, Emile. 1958 [1966]. « Les verbes délocutifs ». *Studia philologica et litteraria in honorem L. Spitzer* ediderunt Anna G. Hatcher et K. L. Selig, 5-63. Bern: Francke [Repris dans Benveniste, Emile. 1966. *Problèmes de linguistique générale*, I, p. 277-285. Paris: Gallimard].

Cahen, Claude. 1962 [1977]. « Contribution à l'étude des impôts dans l'Egypte médiévale », *Journal of the economic and social history of the Orient*, V, 3, p. 244-278 [Repris dans Cahen, Claude. 1977. *Makhzūmiyyāt. Etudes sur l'histoire économique et financière de l'Egypte médiévale*, p. 22-56. Brill, Leiden].

Gacek, Adam (2006). « Abbreviations » , *EALL*, vol. I A-Ed, p. 1-5.

EALL = *Encyclopedia of Arabic Language and Linguistics*, edited by Kees Versteegh (General Editor), Mushira Eid, Alaa Elgibali, Manfred Woidich and Andrzej Zaborski. 2006-2009. Leiden: Brill.

Edzard, Lutz (2007). « La morpho-syntaxe de l'annexion, des formations compositionnelles et des syncrétismes dans les langues sémitiques modernes : analyse contrastive de nouveaux développements », dans Philippe Cassuto et Pierre Larcher (eds) *La formation des mots dans les langues sémitiques*, p. 112-147. Aix-en-Provence : Publications de l'Université de Provence.

EI[2] = *Encyclopédie de l'islam*, 2ème édition, tomes I-XII, 1960-2006. Leiden : Brill.

Fleisch, Henri. 1968. *L'arabe classique: Esquisse d'une structure linguistique*. Nouvelle édition, revue et augmentée. Beyrouth: Dar el-Machreq Editeurs.

Fleisch, Henri. 1979. *Traité de Philologie arabe. Vol. II: Pronoms, morphologie verbale, particules*. Beyrouth: Dar el-Machreq Editeurs.

Hussein, Taha. 1974. *Le Livre des jours*. Traduit de l'arabe par Jean Lecerf et Gaston Wiet. Préface d'André Gide. Paris : Gallimard.

Larcher, Pierre. 1983. « Dérivation délocutive, grammaire arabe, grammaire arabisante et grammaire de l'arabe ». *Arabica* 30:3.246-266.

Larcher, Pierre. 1985. « Vous avez dit 'délocutif'? ». *Langages* 80.99-124.

Martinet, André (1972[1960]). *Eléments de linguistique générale*. Paris : Armand Colin [1ère édition, 1960].

Rey-Debove, Josette. 1975. « Benveniste et l'autonymie: les verbes délocutifs ». *Travaux de linguistique et littérature* 12:1.245-251. Strasbourg.

Shivtiel, Avihai. 1995. « *Fanqalah/fanāqil*. – A nonce-word in Ṭāhā Ḥusayn's *al-Ayyām* », *Journal of Semitic Studies*, XL / 2, Autumn 1995, p. 317-318.

Stetkevych, Jaroslav. 1970. *The Modern Arabic Literary Language. Lexical and Stylistic Developments*. Chicago : Chicago University Press.

The Expression of Deontic Modality in the North-Eastern Neo-Aramaic Dialects

Geoffrey Khan, Cambridge

Abstract
In this paper I shall describe various constructions that are used in North-Eastern Neo-Aramaic (NENA) dialects for the expression of deontic modality. These all convey an element of will and express various degrees of intention, obligation, request, and permission regarding a future action. The examples will be taken from one representative dialect of the group, namely the dialect of Barwar. This was spoken by a community of Assyrian Christians in a cluster of villages in the region of Barwar-i Bala in northern Iraq along the Be-Xelapa river between Amedia and the Turkish border, until the destruction of the villages during the *ʾAnfāl* campaign against the Kurds in the 1980s.

1.0. Irrealis Verbal Forms

In the NENA dialects the finite prefix and suffix conjugations of earlier Aramaic have been completely replaced by participles. Broadly speaking, constructions based on the passive participle came to be used to express the past perfective, replacing the suffix conjugation, and constructions based on the active particle replaced the prefix conjugation. The preliminary stages of this development are already visible in some of the earlier literary forms of eastern Aramaic, such Syriac, Babylonian Talmudic Aramaic and Mandaic, in which the active participle expresses the realis imperfective, whereas the prefix conjugation was largely restricted to the expression of irrealis modality or the future. In NENA the active participle has been extended also into the domain of irrealis and future. In order to distinguish realis from irrealis, most dialects have developed innovative prefixes for the realis form and the unmarked active participle expresses the irrealis.

1.1. Irrealis *qaṭəl* form

The deontic verb forms that are reflexes of the active participles (stem I *qaṭəl*, stem II *mqaṭəl*, stem III *maqṭəl*) without any prefixed particles are referred to for convenience as the *qaṭəl* form. The deontic *qaṭəl* form generally has perfective aspect. In most cases it presents the action as a com-

complete event with a start and endpoint. Sometimes it does not have a clearly delimited endpoint, but it must have a start point future to the present moment. In some contexts, however, the form is used with an imperfective aspect. In what follows the main focus will be on deontic verbs in main clauses.

Main clause verbs in the first person used in a deontic function generally express the intention of the speaker, e.g.

(1) ***ʾázən ʾóðən*** *qázəd d-àwwa gə̀ppa.*ˈ 'I shall go and make towards this cave.' (A39:3)[1]

(2) *ʾâna har-**ṣálən** mðìta*ˈ *mɛ́θən ʾixàla*ˈ *ʾu-**ʾàθena.***ˈ 'I shall just go down to the town to bring food and shall come back.' (A26:30)

In the verb *ʾmr* 'to say' the modality can be interpreted as expressing either intention or a request for permission from the hearer:

(3) *ʾamrə̀nnəx xá-məndi.*ˈ 'I shall tell you something./Let me tell you something.' (A4:15)

(4) *ʾamrə́xlux xà-mdi xéna.*ˈ 'We shall tell you something else./Let us tell you something else.' (A39:8)

Questions in the *qaṭəl* forms such as (5 – 8) are deontic expressions whereby the speaker addresses the hearer expecting him to impose an obligation (deontic necessity) or give permission (deontic possibility):

(5) *mó ʾamràna?*ˈ 'What should/can I say?' (A26:33)

(6) *mò ʾawðéna ʾâna hadîya?*ˈ 'What should/can I do now?' (A26:13)

(7) *mó ʾàwəð?*ˈ 'What should/can he do?' (A28:20)

(8) *lɛ̀ka ʾazéxi?*ˈ 'Where should we go?' (A26:18)

Deontic *qaṭəl* forms in the 2nd and 3rd person express a variety of types of will on the part of the speaker, including request, recommendation and permission, e.g.

---

1 References after the examples relate to the text corpus in Khan (2008). In the transcription a grave accent (v̀) indicates the nuclear stress of the intonation group and an acute accent (v́) marks a non-nuclear stress. An intonation group boundary is marked by the symbol ˈ.

(9) *ʾáxtu kúllɛxu ʾazîtu bɛ̀θa.*ˈ 'All of you should go home.' (A8:85)
(10) *yába hàyyo,*ˈ *ʾaθìtu.*ˈ *čìdetu.*ˈ 'Come, you (are requested to) come. You are invited.' (A7:3)
(11) *ʾámrət ṭla-màlka.*ˈ 'You should say to the king …' (A1:6)
(12) *ʾázət táwrux pɛrmə̀tle.*ˈ 'You should go and slaughter your ox.' (A7:2)
(13) *xúwwe ʾázəl dúke dìye.*ˈ 'Let the snake go to its place.' (A1:8)
(14) *xà-bena ʾázi náše.*ˈ 'People should go (only) once.' (B15:91)
(15) *kút-yom pálṭət ʾu-xàðrət,*ˈ *ʾáṣərta ʾáθət bɛ̀θa.*ˈ 'Every day go out and wander about and then in the evening come back home.' (A14:62)
(16) *hàtxa ʾoðéti b-náše!*ˈ 'This is what you should do to people!' (A22:47)

The use of the form to express iterative actions as in (15) and (16) demonstrates that in some contexts it may express imperfective aspect. The various deontic expressions described above can be negated, e.g.

(17) *ʾána là-ʾaθən mə́nnux.*ˈ 'I shall not come with you.' (A6:6)
(18) *là-ʾawrən gu-máθa.*ˈ 'I shall not go into the village.' (A25:34)
(19) *là-mṣawθət!*ˈ 'Do not speak!' (A26:89)
(20) *là-daqrət bîye.*ˈ 'Do not touch him.' (A26:74)
(21) *la-ʾáθət ṭ-áwðət čù-məndi.*ˈ '(There is no requirement for) you to come and do anything.' (A28:22)
(22) *ʾáp-xa mənnɛ́xu la-ʾàmər:*ˈ *ʾána múθyənna Bə́lbəl Hazàr.*ˈ 'None of you should say "I have brought back Bəlbəl Hazar."' (A8:82)
(23) *ʾáp-xa la-jáwəj mən-gu-ʾAmedìa.*ˈ 'Let nobody move from Amedia.' (A25:27)

Deontic *qaṭəl* forms may be preceded by various preverbal particles:

(i) *xoš*
The particle *xoš* is in origin the imperative of the verb *rxš* 'to go'. It is most frequently attested with verbs with 3rd person subjects, though it can be used with all persons. Examples:

(24) *ʾu-bɛ́θux xoš-ʾàqəð*ˈ 'and may your house burn down' (A17:6)
(25) *xoš-ʾáθa ʾàp-anna*ˈ 'Let them also come back' (B8:4)
(26) *bas-ʾɛ́ni t-xzéla ʾày xoš-ʾáza gu-jahànnam.*ˈ 'But let my eye, which saw her, go to hell.' (A16:2)

It is placed before the negative particle *la* in negative deontic expressions, e.g.

(27) *xóš la-ʾàθe!*ˈ 'Let him not come!'

(ii) *də-, de-*
The particle *də-/de-* may be related to the adverbial particle *diya* 'now'. It is more frequently attested as a prefix to imperative forms than to deontic *qaṭəl* forms.

(28) *də-mjămə́xlən jarrèta.*ˈ *ʾázəx xá-mdita xèta.*ˈ 'Let's put together a food-bag for ourselves. Let's go to another town.' (A30:41)
(29) *ʾu-ʾáti də-ráqðət šɛšátla gànəx.*ˈ 'You should dance and shake yourself.' (A27:11)

It is placed before the negative particle *la* in negated deontic expressions, e.g.

(30) *ʾáti də-la-dàmxeti!*ˈ 'Do not sleep!' (A29:19)
(31) *ʾámər ham-ma-yxàləf,*ˈ *ʿAbda-Raḥmā̃n də-la-ʾàrəq.*ˈ 'He said "That's all right, (only) don't let ʿAbda-Raḥmān get away."' (A23:30)
(32) *ʾálaha də-là-ʾawəð!*ˈ 'God forfend!' (A27:37)

The particle may be combined with *xoš*, e.g.

(33) *də-xoš-gàwra.*ˈ 'Let her marry.' (A26:79)

(iii) *šut*
As with the other particles, this occurs in both positive and negative deontic expressions, e.g.

(34) *ʾən-maṣya šut-ʾoðala.* 'If she can, let her do it.' (C1:11)
(35) *šút la-ʾàθe!*ˈ 'Let him not come!'

1.2. Deontic Expressions with the Verb 'To Be'
In indicative contexts the verb 'to be' is generally expressed by a copula or existential particle. In deontic contexts, however, these are usually replaced by the *qaṭəl* form of the root *hwy*. Some examples of deontic usages in main clauses are:

(1) *háwət basīma ràba.*ˈ 'May you be very well.' (A5:7)
(2) *háwət hášyər ʾītlən jə̀nne.*ˈ 'Be careful, we have jinn.' (A22:26)
(3) *ya-ʾàlaha,*ˈ *háwe ṣáxi hál-ʾɛ-gət ʾána máṭyən ʾə̀lle dìye.*ˈ 'Oh God, let him be well until I reach him.' (A26:80)

This also applies to the expression *la hoya* 'It should not be', 'It is not allowed', 'It is not possible', e.g.

(4) *lá-hoya yóma qamáya xə̀tna t-xazéla kʸàlo.*ˈ 'It is not allowed for the groom to see the bride on the first day.' (A4:36)
(5) *yəmmi la-hòya*ˈ *ʾàna*ˈ *xàθi lá-ʾazən xazə̀nna.*ˈ 'It is impossible for me not to go and find my sister' (A37:9)
(6) *sab-lá-hoya biš-pθìθa.*ˈ 'It (the space between the beams) should not be wider.' (B5:189)

Questions in the *qaṭəl* forms such as (7) and (8) are deontic expressions whereby the speaker addresses the hearer expecting him to impose an obligation (deontic necessity) or give permission (deontic possibility):

(7) *de-màṭo hóya?*ˈ 'How can it be/should it be?' (A30:21)
(8) *mò-hoyali gwárta-w?*ˈ 'What can marriage be to me?' (A16:5)

In various constructions expressing wishes, a deontic form of the verb *hwy* is omitted. This is found in the following contexts:

(i) Exclamations
(9) *qə̀ṭma b-rèšux!*ˈ 'May ash be on your head!' (A23:8)
(10) *ʾámər brīxta dudīya ṭ-iwət ʾáti qīma gàwa!*ˈ 'Blessed be the cradle in which you grew up!' (A21:41)

(ii) Expressions that are parenthetical or supplementary tags
(11) *ʾáti qəm-paqðə̀tli,*ˈ *ʾát basíma ràba.*ˈ 'You instructed me—you be well (= thank you).' (A8:50)
(12) *ʾálaha šuxa-l-šə̀mme qəm-mšadə̀rri ʾəčči-u ʾə̀čča dàwe.*ˈ 'God—praise be to his name—sent me ninety-nine gold coins.' (A6:10)
(13) *y-azīwa mšamšīwa bɛθ-qòra,*ˈ *rə̀ḥqa mən-an-dukàne!*ˈ 'They would go and hold a ceremony in the cemetery—(may death be) far from these places!' (B10:3)

2.0. The Future Form *bəd-qaṭəl*

2.1. Deontic Future

The *qaṭəl* form may be combined with the prefixed particle *bəd-* or reduced forms of this (*bt-*, *b-*, *t-*) to express the future. This particle, which is widespread in the NENA dialects, has usually be regarded as a phonetically attenuated form of the verbal construction **baʿe d-* 'he wants to', or **bʿe d-* 'it is desired that' (Nöldeke 1868: 294-296; Pennacchietti 1994a: 281, 1994b: 137; Cohen 1984: 520). This may be used with a predictive or deontic future function. We shall be concerned here with its deontic usage.

When the verb has an agentive 1st singular subject the *bəd-qaṭəl* form generally has a modal sense expressing deontic intention, e.g.

(1) *b-ṣàlyən*ˡ *b-tâpqən bìye.*ˡ 'I shall go down to meet him.' (A4:21)
(2) *ʾàp-ʾana bṱ-ázən šúla*ˡ *pàlxən.*ˡ 'I also shall go and work.' (A23:1)
(3) *b-zonə̂nne b-xamšī dinâre.*ˡ 'I shall buy it for fifty dinars.' (A24:23)
(4) *t-yawə́nnux zùzux.*ˡ 'I shall give you your money.' (A1:10)

The intention may be to perform the action in the immediate future, e.g.

(5) *hadīya b-zadrànna gâni.*ˡ 'Now I am going to shake myself.' (A24:27)

When expressing deontic intention the *bəd-qaṭəl* form is occasionally combined with the particle of immediacy *də-/de-*, e.g.

(6) *ʾána də-ṱ-amrə̂nnox ʾó-mdi-t taxrə̀nne.*ˡ 'I shall tell you what I remember.' (B15:1)
(7) *pálgət dáwi de-t-yánne ʾə̂lle dīye.*ˡ 'I shall give him half of my gold.' (A14:92)

When the verb has an agentive 1st plural subject, the form often has a cohortative modal sense (Let's ...), e.g.

(8) *bṱ-àrqexi.*ˡ 'Let's flee.' (A30:41)
(9) *bas-ṱ-ázexi ṭalbə̂xla m-bába dīya.*ˡ 'But let us go and ask her father for her hand.' (A29:38)
(10) *b-súrəθ lɛ́ðən mú y-amrīle,*ˡ *ṱ-ámrəx mtagəbràna.*ˡ 'I do not know what they call it in *surəθ*, let's say "governor."' (B6:47)

The form may express deontic obligation. In such cases the verb generally has an agentive 2nd person subject, e.g.

(11) *ʾati bṭ-àzet.*ˡ 'You should go.' (A8:46)
(12) *ṭ-azîtu qam-d-o-gə̀ppa,*ˡ *ʾaw-gə́ppa rába ramànɛle.*ˡ *b-qarìtu:*ˡ *ʾó Bə́lbəl Hazàr!*ˡ 'You should go to the cave, the cave is very high. You should cry "Oh Bəlbəl Hazar."' (A8:28)
(13) *b-zɛ̀nət*ˡ *gótət d-an-xoránux xène*ˡ *ʾu-b-qàrət.*ˡ *ṭ-ámrət ʾó Bə́lbəl Hazàr!*ˡ 'You should stand next to the others, your friends, and call out. You should say "Oh Bəlbəl Hazar!"' (A8:48)

2.2. The Functional Distinction between Deontic *qaṭəl* and *bəd-qaṭəl*
The *bəd-qaṭəl* form is more frequently used to express a prediction of the future than as a deontic form. The *qaṭəl* form may also express a predictive future, but only where the speaker is not completely certain about it and is not guaranteeing that it will be fulfilled. This is shown by the fact that the *qaṭəl* predictive future would normally be used after the particle *balki* 'perhaps', e.g.

(1) *bálki ʾáθya tə̀mməl.*ˡ 'Perhaps she will come tomorrow.'
(2) *ṭ-aθya tə̀mməl.*ˡ 'She will (certainly) come tomorrow.'

When used deontically, the two forms are also distinguished functionally by differing degrees of certainty of fulfillment. The *bəd-qaṭəl* is used when the speaker has a high degree of certainty that the desired action will be realized. It is for this reason that the majority of cases of the deontic use of the *bəd-qaṭəl* form are in the 1st person. This reflects the fact that a speaker typically has more control over and so more certainty concerning his own future actions than those of others. It follows from this that when used deontically in other persons, the speaker uses the high degree of certainty of outcome expressed the *bəd-qaṭəl* form as a strategy to add force to a request or command.

2.3. Negation of *bəd-qaṭəl* Forms
The negative particle *la* cannot be combined with the *bəd-qaṭəl* form. To express the negative, a suppletive negative form is used. This is the negation of the *ʾi-qaṭəl* form, with the prefix *ʾi-*, which normally expresses imperfective habitual aspect (*la-y-qaṭəl*). There are various phonetic vari-

ants of the *la-y-qaṭəl* form, which exhibit various degrees of contaction, viz. *le-y-qaṭəl, lɛ-qaṭəl*, e.g.

(1) *lè-y-axlena.*ˈ 'I shall not eat.' (B5:35)
(2) *ˀána m-axxa-húdxa lè-y-azən.*ˈ 'I shall not go beyond here.' (A12:23)
(3) *ˀána là-y-asqən.*ˈ 'I shall not go up.' (A32:29)
(4) *bas-lè-y-yənna bnáθi-llɛxu.*ˈ 'But I shall not give my daughters to you.' (A12:17)

As remarked, the *ˀi-qaṭəl* form is used elsewhere to express imperfective habitual aspect. The positive *bəd-qaṭəl* form is, however, intrinsically perfective. The explanation appears to be that the positive future perfective form asserts that a specific action will (predictive) or is desired to (deontic) take place at a particular point in time whereas its negated form should properly be interpreted as expressing an enduring property of the subject referent rather than referring to an event that is bound to a particular point in time. When a speaker says *ṭ-axlən* 'I shall eat', he is asserting that there will be a particular point in time when he will eat. When he says *le-y-axlən*, on the other hand, the sense is 'I have the property of not eating'. The salience of the particular point in time of an action is diffused when it is negated to the extent that an imperfective form is used.

3.0. The Imperative Form

3.1. Commands and Prohibitions

In most cases the imperative form is used perfectively to command the performance of a single delimited action with a clear start and endpoint, e.g.

(1) *prúmu rèše!*ˈ 'Cut off his head!' (A24:31)
(2) *hallúle ˀálpa dàwe!*ˈ 'Give him a thousand gold pieces!' (A1:14)
(3) *šqúlla yalə̀xθa!*ˈ 'Take the scarf!' (A4:18)
(4) *diya-mɛ́θu júlli malušùla!*ˈ 'Now bring my clothes and put them on (me)!' (A4:20)
(5) *wúð ða-spayúθa mə̀nni!*ˈ 'Do me a favour!' (A7:17)
(6) *háyyo ṣlī Kărīm ˀáti gu-d-áwwa balùˁa.*ˈ 'Come Karim, go down into this conduit!' (A14:16)

Prohibitions may be expressed by negating an imperative form by the negative particle *la*. If this particle is combined with the verb in a stress group it typically takes the stress, e.g.

(7) *lá-wuð qàla!*ˈ 'Do not make a noise!' (A30:44)
(8) *lá-mur hàtxa!*ˈ 'Do not say that!' (A26:52)
(9) *bróni là qəṭlúle!*ˈ 'Do not kill my son!' (A33:6)
(10) *là maštóla mĩya*ˈ 'Do not give them water to drink!' (A25:9)

When two prohibitions expressed by imperative forms occur in a series of two closely connected clauses, the negative particle is sometimes gapped in the second clause, e.g.

(11) *lá-wuð hàtxa*ˈ *qṭúl ʾanna-bnónə nâše kùlla.*ˈ 'Don't do that, don't kill all the people.' (A29:17)

On some occasions the imperative is used to command or prohibit a less clearly delimited action. In (12) and (13), for example, the imperatives 'work!' and 'search!' respectively clearly command the inception of the action but do not necessarily imply an endpoint. In (14) the actions commanded by the imperatives are most easily interpreted as iterative. The speaker is referring to the annual custom of Kurds to bring sheep into the village during transhumance and intends his command to apply to all future years.

(12) *xuš-plùxən!*ˈ *ta-mú-t baṭila ṫiwa gu-bɛ̀θa?*ˈ 'Go and work! Why are you sitting idly in the house?' (A39:1)
(13) *ṭó-lɛxu xa-šúla ta-t-xǎ́yitu bìye!*ˈ 'Search for a job for yourselves by which you may make a living!' (A30:1)
(14) *lá-masqu l-gârət ʾùmra!*ˈ *m-gu-gârət ʾúmra hóla náblula tămáha rə̀ḥqa!*ˈ *ṭla-mótu mɛθóyəlla gârət ʾùmra?*ˈ 'Don't take them onto the roof of the church. Take them far away from the roof of the church. Why do you bring them on the roof of the church?' (B18:7)

In (15) and (16) the imperatives are negated by the particle *bassa* 'enough!' and command the end of an activity that is already in progress without any implied starting point:

(15) *bâssa bxɛ̀gən*ˈ *bâssa wuð-tàzi.*ˈ 'Do not weep any more! Do not mourn any more!' (A26:88)
(16) *bâssa štî ʾu-rwì!*ˈ 'Don't drink any more and get any more drunk!'

On numerous occasions the imperative is preceded by the particle of immediacy *də-/de-*. Most attested examples are positive commands, e.g.

(17) *də-šqúl ʾanna-zùze!*ˈ 'Take these coins!' (A1:27)
(18) *də-šùqla!*ˈ 'Leave it!' (A5:7)
(19) *de-mùrri!*ˈ 'Tell me!' (A4:26)
(20) *de-wúr gu-d-áwwa gùrba!*ˈ 'Go into this torso!' (A14:67)

As has been discussed above, also the 2nd person of the *qaṭəl* form can be used deontically to express commands or prohibitions. This may be used perfectively to express single delimited actions, e.g.

(21) *ʾázət táwrux pɛrmə̀tle.*ˈ 'You should go and slaughter your ox.' (A7:2)

It may also be used to express general commands or prohibitions that are not delimited to a single action, e.g.

(22) *hàtxa ʾoðéti b-nâše!*ˈ 'This is what you should do to people!' (A22:47)

The distinction between the imperative form and the deontic *qaṭəl* form, therefore, is not primarily one of aspect, although this may have some bearing on the choice between the two. The main factor is rather the communicative profile of the command. In principle a speaker uses the imperative when he wishes to give the command a high degree of salience. The deontic *qaṭəl* form is used when it has a lesser degree of salience. Various features contribute to this salience. One feature is immediacy. All other things being equal, an imperative expresses the will of the speaker for an action to be performed closer to the present moment than the *qaṭəl* form. Consider, for example, the pair of constructions (23) and (24), both of which are perfective in aspect. In (23) the speaker invites the addressee to come immediately and join him swimming. In (24) the request relates to an action of coming at a point further in the future:

(23) *ʾána hon-sxáya gàwa.*ˡ *bǎyət ṯ-áθyət sàxyət?*ˡ *də-háyyo sxà!*ˡ 'I am swimming in it. Do you want to swim? Come and swim!' (A25:61)
(24) *yómət ṭḷàθa,*ˡ *ʾáθət kəslɛ̀ni.*ˡ 'In three days time come to us.' (A22:17)

It is relevant to note that the particle of immediacy *də-/de-*, which is commonly used with imperatives but only sporadically with deontic *qaṭəl*, is likely to be related etymologically to the adverbial *diya* 'now'. In some NENA dialects it is used in progressive constructions that express actions that are taking place at the present moment (e.g. C. Ankawa *də-k-šatən* 'I am drinking').

As we have seen in (12) and (13), the action commanded by an imperative may extend indefinitely into the future. In (15) the action has no definite starting point. The relevant feature in all these cases is that the speaker commands the action to begin or end immediately.

The use of the imperative to express the command of iterative actions cannot be motivated by temporal immediacy. The salience of the command arises from its high degree of force, which is greater than in corresponding iterative deontic expressions with *qaṭəl* forms such as (25):

(25) *kút-yom pálṭət ʾu-xàðrət,*ˡ *ʾáṣərta ʾáθət bɛ̀θa.*ˡ 'Every day go out and wander about and then in the evening come back home.' (A14:62)

Another feature that contributes to salience appears to be the positiveness of the command. All other things being equal, there is a greater tendency to use the deontic *qaṭəl* form with a negative command than with a positive one, as reflected in (26) and (27), in which positive commands and prohibitions with perfective aspect referring to immediate actions are used side by side:

(26) *mə̀ra hàyyo,*ˡ *hàyyo!*ˡ *madam-ṯ-ĩwət ʾàti,*ˡ *hàyyo!*ˡ *là-ʾazət.*ˡ 'Come, come. Since it is you, come, don't go!' (A24:36)
(27) *ʾáti là pálxət.*ˡ *ʾáti tù.*ˡ *ʾàna pálxən.*ˡ 'Don't you work. You sit down. I shall work.' (A21:23)

Indeed, in some NENA dialects, such as Qaraqosh, negative commands can only be expressed by negating the *qaṭəl* form (cf. Khan 2002: 351). In Barwar, as in many other NENA dialects, negation has been extended to imperative forms, but the distribution of negated commands is still less than that of positive commands on account of the inherently lower degree of salience of a negated command. The fact that the particle *də-/de-*, which gives added salience to a command, is largely restricted to positive commands may be a further reflection of this inherently lower salience of negated commands. It is also relevant to recall here the asymmetry between the positive future form *bəd-qaṭəl* and the negated future *la-y-qaṭəl*, which has the form of a habitual imperfective.

All the uses of the imperative described above can be reconciled with the claim that the form is perfective. As already remarked, cases such as (12), (13) and (15) can be regarded as having an ingressive or terminative sense, which are features exhibited by other perfective forms. The occurrence of the imperative in iterative expressions can be explained as being the use of a perfective form appropriate to command an individual occurrence of the iterated action to command, by implication, the iterated action as a whole. It can be said that the basic perfectivity of the imperative form, which gives the commanded action delimited boundaries, results in its salience and it is this perfectivity that gives the sense of greater force in the command. The deontic *qaṭəl* form, on the other hand, may express either perfective or imperfective aspect. We may summarize the features contributing to the salience in imperative forms in the scales below, in which the symbol > should be read as 'more salient than'. All other things being equal, a command with the features on the lefthand side of the scales would be more likely to be expressed by an imperative than those with the features on the righthand side:

Perfective	>	Imperfective
Positive	>	Negative
Immediate	>	Non-immediate

The imperative may be extended by a variety of suffixes. These include:
With the singular imperative:

-ga
-ən, -ena
-gən, -gena

With the plural imperative

-gu

Examples of suffixes added to *pluṭ* 'go out! (sing.) and *pluṭu* 'go out! (pl.)':

plúṭga
plúṭən *plúṭena*
plúṭgən *plúṭgena*

plúṭugu

Informants feel that these suffixes add additional force to the command like the prefixed particle *də-/de-*. It is significant that they are attested only with positive commands, which is likely to be a reflection of the inherently lower salience of the negative commands. Another factor that determines the distribution of the imperative forms with added suffixes is their position within a section of discourse. When there are two or more imperatives in a sequence, forms with added suffixes tend to be placed at the end of the sequence. The heavy morphological coding of the forms is used in such contexts to mark a final boundary of a discourse unit. The sequence may consist of two or more different imperatives in a closely knit unit as in (28–30) or the repetition of the same imperative as in (31) and (32), e.g.

(28) *dúṛu sógena kəs-babàxu*ˈ 'Return, go to your father' (A14:85)
(29) *xuš-plùxən!*ˈ 'Go and work!' (A39:1)
(30) *qu-pέgən kàde*ˈ 'Get up and bake kade cakes' (A30:41)
(31) *sī́-mur ta-pə̀llən wazī̀r*ˈ *múrgena málka θèle.*ˈ ''Go and and say to the minister so-and-so, say the king has come back.' (A4:33)
(32) *xùl!*ˈ *dànεla.*ˈ *qìrra.*ˈ *xùlena!*ˈ 'Eat! It is time. It has got cold. Eat!' (B5:34)

Another strategy for giving added force to an imperative is to increase the grammatical coding by combining the imperative form with an independent 2nd person pronoun. This is generally placed after the imperative, e.g.

(33) *qu-plúṭ ʾàti*ˈ *xzi-mò-d-ila qə̀ṣṣət.*ˈ 'Go out and see what is happening.' (A26:54)
(34) *túgən ʾáti gàwe*ˈ 'Sit in it!' (A20:3)
(35) *hâyyo ṣlī́ Kăr̄ìm ʾáti gu-d-âwwa balù*ʿ*a.*ˈ 'Come Karim, go down into this conduit.' (A14:16)

The imperatives of the verbs *qym* 'to get up' and *ʾtw* 'to sit down' are often combined with the resultative participle: *qu-qīma!* 'Get up (ms.)!', *qu-qīmta!* (fs.), *tu-ṭīwa!* 'Sit down (ms.)!', *tu-ṭīwta!* 'Sit down (fs.)!' In the plural, the plural inflection is used only on the participle: *qu-qīme!* 'Get up (pl.)!'; *tu-ṭīwe!* 'Sit down (pl.)'. In some cases the plural of the imperative element *qu-* or *tu-* is dispensed with altogether and the plural participle is used alone with imperative function, e.g.

(36) *páqðu tìwe.*ˡ 'Please, sit down.' (A15:8)
(37) *mə̀ra de-ṭìwe.*ˡ 'She said "Sit down."' (A21:28)
(38) *qīme so-mὲθole ʾəlli-ḍìyi.*ˡ 'Get up and go and bring him to me.' (A7:7)

3.2. Narrative Imperative

In a few cases the imperative is used in narrative as a substitute for a perfective narrative verbal form. These are addressed to the person performing the action and are typically used when there is a transition between spatial locations that involves a verb of movement. The clause containing the imperative may open with a 3rd person subject pronoun as in (1) and (2):

(1) *qīmtɛla zìlta,*ˡ *muθέθəlla quṣárta ḍìya.*ˡ *ʾa-zórta muttáθəlla gu-d-έ quṣártət šwàwe*ˡ *ʾu-nubàltəlla.*ˡ *haḍìya,*ˡ *ʾáw* ***qu-šqúlla*** *quṣàrta-w*ˡ *sī be-šwàwux.*ˡ *šlắma-llɛxu šwàwe.*ˡ 'She went and brought her cooking pot. She put the small one in the cooking pot of the neighbours and took it (to her husband). Now, he — get up and take the cooking pot and go to the house of your neighbour! "Greeings to you neighbours."' (A5:4)

(2) *qâyəm yawə̀lle ʾálpa dâwe xène.*ˡ *ʾáw xá-reša m-tâma* ***qú-si*** *l-bὲθa.*ˡ *ʾáp ʾan-tre-ʾálpe dâwe xéne* ***mὲθila.***ˡ *ʾu-****háyyo*** *šlắma-llux xóni xùwwe!*ˡ 'He gives him another thousand gold pieces. He — directly from there get up and go home. Bring back also those two thousand pieces of gold and come back "Greetings my brother snake! Peace and blessings!"' (A1:19-20)

Example (3) illustrates the use of an imperative for another type of narrative strategy. The negated imperative of the verb to say *lá-mur* 'Do not say!', which is presumably addressed to the hearer of the narrative, has the function of drawing special attention to what follows.

(3) *ʾu-lá-mur qáyəθ b-o-ṱ-ìle də̀pne.*ˡ 'Guess what, (literally: Don't say) he knocked into the one next to him.' (A22:34)

4.0. Constructions with *ʾə̀lla*

The particle *ʾə̀lla* is a contraction of the conditional particle *ʾən* and the negator *la,* with the stress on the conditional particle rather than the negator. This is used in clauses that come after a negated main clause. A clause introduced by *ʾə̀lla* typically expresses new information with discourse prominence, whereas the main clause before it is bound to the preceding context in some way, e.g.

(1) *b-ču-ʾúrxa ʾo-Dəmdə́ma lɛ́ šaqḷitule*ˡ *ʾə̀lla qăṭitula mĭiyət Dəmdə̀ma.*ˡ 'By no means will you capture Dəmdəma unless you cut off the water of Dəmdəma.' (A11:17)

(2) *xə̀tna lè-y-axəl*ˡ *ʾə̀lla qablìle xà-məndi.*ˡ 'The groom would not eat unless they pledged something to him.' (B10:40)

(3) *ʾána mĭrtɛwən le-y-ʾáθyən b-xábrət čù-ʾurza,*ˡ *ʾə̀lla ṱ-áθya báxta maθyàli.*ˡ 'I said that I would not come by the word of any man, unless a woman came to fetch me.' (A8:94)

On some occasions the content of a clause introduced by *ʾə̀lla* is given in the preceding context, but the speaker uses the construction to give the clause enhanced prominence. It is typically used when the speaker wishes to insist forcefully that something be done, e.g.

(4) *ʾən-lá galə̀tli ʾánna šaqyáθa módi gu-rèšux,*ˡ *ʾánna brinánət mòdila*ˡ … *ʾən-là galə̀tli,*ˡ *ʾána lɛ̀-qɛṣənne káwsux.*ˡ … *là qɛṣə̀nne káwsux,*ˡ *ʾə̀lla ṱ-amrə̀tli ʾánna ma-brinànela gu-réšux.*ˡ 'If you do not reveal what these scars on your head are, what these wounds are from … if you do not reveal this to me, I shall not cut your hair … I shall not cut your hair, unless you tell me what these wounds are on your head.' (A29:5-6)

Clauses expressing insistence that open with *ʾə̀lla* are sometimes used with deontic force independently of a preceding main clause, e.g.

(5) *kĭzla bĭiye dìye,*ˡ *mə̀ra ʾə̀lla gáwrət.*ˡ 'They tried (to persuade) him and said "You must marry."' (A16:6)

(6) *mə̀re lá b-àlaha,*ˡ *ʾə̀lla maṣlə̀nnəx ʾàna.*ˡ 'No, by God. I shall take you down.' (A29:27)

(7) *mə́ra là*ˈ *ˀána har-bṯ-àzən.*ˈ *ˀə́lla xazyánne xòni.*ˈ 'No. I shall still go. I must see my brother.' (A8:66)

Insistence on a prohibition may be expressed by using a construction opening with *ˀən-lá* independently of a main clause, paralleling the use of *ˀə́lla* to express insistence on a command, e.g.

(8) *ˀá-ṣəpra ˀī́la ròxi,*ˈ *ˀən-lá qaṭlī́le ˀo-táwrət wàla,*ˈ *šaqlī́le ˀo-ṣə̀pra.*ˈ 'That sparrow is my spirit. They must not kill that wild ox and take that sparrow.' (A12:41)

5.0. Passive

Deontic possibility or obligation may be expressed by passive constructions consisting of the verb *ˀθy* 'to come' and an infinitive, e.g.

(1) *ˀáy qəṣṣə́tta rī̀xtɛla.*ˈ *la-ˀáθya l-mtanòye.*ˈ 'It is a long story. It cannot be told.' (A25:52)

(2) *mə́ra mòdi qə́ṣṣət?*ˈ *tànilɛni!*ˈ *mə́re là*ˈ *lɛ-ˀáθya mtanòye*ˈ *xā̃f nâše šmàˀəllɛni.*ˈ 'They said "What is the story? Tell us!" He said "No. It cannot/must not be told, lest people are listening to us."' (A35:10-11)

References

Cohen, D., 1984, *La phrase nominale et l'évolution du système verbal en sémitique. Etudes de syntaxe historique*, Paris.

Khan, G., 2008, *The Neo-Aramaic Dialect of Barwar*. Leiden—Boston.

Nöldeke, T., 1868, *Grammatik der Neusyrischen Sprache am Urmia-See und in Kurdistan*, Leipzig.

Pennacchietti, F., 1994a, 'Il preterito neoaramacio con pronome oggetto', *Zeitschrift der Deutschen Morgenländischen Gesellschaft* 144, pp. 259-283.

Pennacchietti, F., 1994b, 'I preverbi del passato in semitico', in V. Brugnatelli (ed.), *Sem Cam Iafet: Atti della 7ª Giornata Studi Camito-Semitici e Indeurope*, Milan, pp. 133-150.

Injunctive Protases and the Grammaticalisation of Elliptic Conditional Clauses in Semitic*

Lutz Edzard, University of Oslo

Abstract

In this paper, I will address the issue of a formal (modal-deontic) feature in Akkadian treaty texts and other documents, namely the injunctive *šumma (lā)* clauses (oath clauses/Schwursätze). More specifically, I will investigate the grammaticalisation of elliptic conditional – positive and negative – *šumma (lā)* clauses which function as polite hyperbolic imperatives in the sense of oath clauses. "Elliptic" here refers to the assumed lack of a (direct) apodosis in such sentences. The paper will also address the grammaticalisation of irreal conditional particles as optative/ injunctive markers (if this direction indeed represents the diachronic development) in the wider Semitic context. The comparable distribution of injunctive protases which can stand by themselves, one the one hand, and injunctive forms (notably imperatives) on the other hand, is the main point of this paper.

1 Introduction

Among the formal or, if one so pleases, "polite" features in Akkadian treaty texts one finds the individual clauses or "paragraphs" of the treaty introduced by the conditional marker *šumma (lā)*. Normally, this conditional marker introduces the protasis of a conditional sentence, as in legal texts like the Codex Hammurabi. However, the particle *šumma* is also widely attested in oath sentences (cf. von Soden 1995: 293 (= § 185g–i)) and Huehnergard 2005: 437f. (= § 36.3)), in which the "Boolean" value of the sentence is seemingly inverted. Thus, *šumma* introduces negative statements ("may not") and *šumma lā* positive statements ("may"). Here are three examples of such inverted positive statements:

(1) *šumma aḫī Purattim gulgullātim lā umalli*
'I will fill the banks of the Euphrates with skulls' =
"if I won't fill the banks of the Euphrates with skulls,
<<negative consequence>>"

(2) *šumma … lā umalli u lā uṣṣiṣ* 'I shall … certainly fill and … bend' =
"if I won't fill and bend, <<negative consequence>>"

* Thanks to Werner Diem, Stephan Guth, and Michael P. Streck for comments on an earlier version of this paper. Responsibility remains with the author alone.

(3) *šumma … lā attalk-ak-kim-ma u ṣibût-ki lā ētepuš*
'I will certainly come to you and carry out your wish' =
"if I (will) have not come to you and carried out your wish,
<<negative consequence>>"

As we will further see below, the inherent logic in such clauses probably is that an apodosis à la "may I die" or "may I be cursed" has to be mentally supplied after the respective protasis. In other words: in a diachronic analysis, the oath clauses will be analysed as elliptic conditional sentences.[1] In a synchronic analysis, however, *šumma* and *šumma lā* will be analysed as asseverative particles which can be rendered by 'certainly' and 'certainly not', respectively.

In the following, an attempt will be made to present the synchronic analysis in a comparative Semitic and typological perspective. First, I will show that injunctive forms and protases can appear in comparable syntactical distribution. In a second step, I will assemble data on elliptic (or "defective") conditional clauses (protases) in general, independently of the issue of injunctions. In a further step, I will investigate the question as to which degree conditional markers / conjunctions and asseverative modal-deontic prefixes are etymologically related.

2 Conditional clauses and hyperbolic imperatives

The connection between conditional clauses and / or hyperbolic imperatives, to allude to the title of a paper by Lawler (1975), has not escaped the attention of theoretical linguistics. In this context, it is important to note that conditional structures are not necessarily hypotactic, but may be paratactic as well (cf. also Haiman 1983).[2] Lawler's (1975: 371) examples involving the conjunctions *and* and *or* are:

(4) a. *Open the window and I'll kill you.*
b. *Open the window and I'll kiss you.*
c. *Open the window or I'll kill you.*
d. ?*Open the window or I'll kiss you.*

1 Tietz (1963: 87–90) problematises the term "ellipsis" in this context and operates with the alternative term "brachylogy", as it is not clear *a priori* whether the optative use of certain particles preceded the conditional use, and as "elliptic" structures were not necessarily conceived as such by native Semitic speakers.

2 Diem (2002) makes the same point for complement clauses (e.g., *ʾan yafʿala*).

Obviously, (4)a. could be paraphrased as "if you open the window, I'll kill you", (4)b. as "if you open the window, I'll kiss you" (assuming that being kissed is desirable), and (4)c. as if you don't open the window, I'll kill you. Only (4)d. is semantically ill-formed (still assuming that being kissed is desirable).

German, among many other languages, allows for similar constructions. König (1986: 234) offers the following example, which likewise can be paraphrased by a conditional structure:

(5) *Störe ihn nicht, dann wird er dich auch nicht stören.*

Turning to Semitic, injunctives in the protasis of a conditional structure are also attested in Akkadian. Consider the following example, in which the protasis consists of two precative verb phrases, *līter limṭī-ma* (cf. Huehnergard 2005: 146):

(6) *kaspum līter limṭī-ma ul atâr-ma ul araggam*
'let the silver increase, let it decrease, and I will not contest again' =
"whether the silver increases or decreases, I will not contest again"

Diehl (2004: 100–103 and 331–335) adduces relevant examples from Biblical Hebrew, in which the injunctive forms (mostly imperatives) function as protases:[3]

(7) *zō(ʾ)ṯ ʿăśū wi-ḥyū* (Gen 42:18) 'do this, and you will live' =
"if you do this, you will live"

The second member of such constructions need not be an imperative. One encounters also examples with a consecutive perfect in the second position (the "apodosis", if one so pleases):

(8) *harʾē-nū nā(ʾ) ʾeṯ-məḇō(ʾ) hā-ʿīr wə-ʿāśīnū ʿimmə-ḵā ḥāseḏ* (Judg 1:24)
'show us the way into the city, and we will be loyal to you' =
"if you show us the way into the city, we will be loyal to you"

This phenomenon has also caught the attention of the native Arab grammarians, who commented on structures such as

3 Cf. also GKC 325 (= §110f) and Bergsträsser 1929: 50 (= § 10k).

(9) *uṭlub taǧid* 'search [and] you will / shall find' =
if you search, you will find,[4]

which, according to the native Arab(ic) grammarians, had an underlying representation *ʾin taṭlub taǧid*. According to Sībawayhi, al-Ḫalīl claimed regarding injunctive forms in a protasis position *ʾanna hāḏihī l-ʾawāʾila kulla-hā fī-hā maʿnā ʾin* "that all these first parts [of the sentence] have the inherent meaning 'if'" (Sībawayhi, *Kitāb*, ch. 253, p. 399).[5]

The examples in this section illustrate the ambivalent position of such sentences between paratactic and hypotactic structures: while the surface structure is clearly paratactic, the "underlying" logical form ("deep structure") is hypotactic. This is at least the standard position in the ("Eurocentric") literature that *a priori* associates a hypotactic structure with a conditional sentence. Whether or not this is really the case in Semitic, i.e. whether paratactic structures cannot be equally supposed to be underlying, remains to be seen.

3 Conditional clauses without an apodosis

"Defective" of elliptic conditional clauses (protases) are attested sporadically, irrespectively of whether they convey an injunctive sense or not. Reckendorf (1921: 515f. = § 264.4), among others, devotes some space to the phenomenon of conditional clauses without an apodosis. Here is an example:

(10) *fa-ʾin ʾabat muhāǧiratu qurayšin*
'and if the emigrants from Qurayš are unwilling [, then what?]'

A frequent explanation offered by the grammars of Arabic is that the apodosis is clear anyway in such cases. Pragmatically, such examples are not rare in oral registers of languages. In German, for instance, it is perfectly normal to utter examples as

(11) *Ja, wenn du meinst.*
'Well, if you think so [, do it. (But I have warned you.)].'

4 For thorough discussion cf. Reckendorf 1921: 491f. and Peled 1987.

5 For the topic of conditional clauses in general in the native Arab(ic) tradition cf. Devenyi 1988 and 2007, as well as Versteegh 1991. Cf. also Trumpp 1881.

Relevant examples also appear in the context of disjunctive conditional clauses (cf. Brockelmann 1913: 653 (= § 439)):

(12) *ʾin tamamta ʿalā mā kāna bayn-ī wa-bayna-ka wa-ʾil-lā nāǧaztu-ka*
'if you fulfill our agreements [, it is good];
if not, I shall draw into battle against you'

Renate Jacobi (1967), Bernhard Lewin (1970), and Helmut Gätje (1976), among others, have analysed the type of conditional clauses in which the apodosis does not express a direct consequence of the protasis, but rather reflects a logical break or split ("Bedingungssätze mit [logischer] Verschiebung" in the German grammatical nomenclature). One could also argue that the apodosis proper is missing and that the extant apodosis is really the beginning of a new syntactic period. The best known example in this context emanates from the Joseph story as related in Sūra 12:

(13) *ʾin yasriq fa-qad saraqa ʾaḫun la-hū min qablu* (Q 12:77)
'if he has stolen [, it is not noteworthy, because] already one of his brothers has stolen earlier' (cf. Brockelmann 1913: 645 (= § 430))

The further analysis of this type of "defective" conditional clause with a logical break, however, is not the subject of this paper.

4 The Semitic particle *lū*/*law* and the asseverative prefix *l*- (**la*-)

Before finally turning to the issue of elliptic conditional clauses as polite injunctions, it is necessary to dwell on the etymology of the involved particles. At first sight, it is striking that both the asseverative prefix *l*- (**la*-) and the purpose-inducing prefix (preposition) *li*- on the one hand, and the particle *lū* / *law*, which typically introduces irreal conditions but also can be used in asseverative context, start out with an *l*.[6]

The following chart, which is restricted to the first person sg. (in the case of Amharic) and the third person ms. sg. (in the cases of Arabic, Aramaic, and ESA), is oriented at Huehnergard 1983: 577. The chart ex-

6 Brockelmann (1908: 565 (= § 260) and 1913: 24, 28 (=§§ 14, 15)) contended that *l(v)*- in purpose clauses reflected the original function of *l(v)*- and that precative forms with an *l*-prefix reflected also originally purpose clauses whose main clause was no longer there. Cf. Huehnergard 1983: 577.

poses another seeming coincidence, the *l* in both the asseverative / injunctive particle *l-* and the purpose-introducing particle *li-*:

		Injunctive (*l-*)	Purpose (*li-*)
(14)	Amharic	*lə*C_1C_2*ä*C_3	*l-ə*C_1*ä*C_2C_3
	Arabic	*li-ya*C_1C_2*v*C_3	*li-ya*C_1C_2*v*C_3*a*
	Aramaic	**li*C_1C_2*o*C_3	*lə-yi*C_1C_2*o*C_3
	ESA	*l-y*$C_1C_2C_3$*(n)*	*l-y*$C_1C_2C_3$*(n)*

Note also the Arabic injunctive form *fa-l-ya*C_1C_2*v*C_3 (in connection with the conjunction *fa-*), in which the precative prefix is shortened to *l-*.

The Akkadian precative paradigm looks as follows (here, I give the complete paradigm (3rd and 1st ps.) with {p-r-s} as a basis and the corresponding preterite forms in parentheses – cf. Huehnergard 1983: 586 and Testen 1993: 1). Note the special 3rd f. sg. form in the Assyrian paradigm:[7]

(15)	Babylonian		Assyrian	
	G-stem	D-stem	G-stem	D-stem
3 c.sg.	*liprus* (*iprus*)	*liparris* (*uparris*)	—	—
3 m.sg.			*liprus* (*iprus*)	*luparris* (*uparris*)
3 f.sg.	—	—	*lu taprus* (*taprus*)	*lu tuparris* (*tuparris*)
1 c.sg.	*luprus* (*aprus*)	*luparris* (*uparris*)	*laprus* (*aprus*)	*luparris* (*uparris*)
3 m.pl.	*liprusū* (*iprusū*)	*liparrissū* (*uparrisū*)	*liprusū* (*iprusū*)	*luparrissū* (*uparrisū*)
3 f.pl.	*liprusā* (*iprusā*)	*liparrissā* (*uparrisā*)	*liprusā* (*iprusā*)	*luparrissā* (*uparrisā*)
1 c.pl.	*i niprus* (*niprus*)	*i nuparris* (*nuparris*)	*lu niprus* (*niprus*)	*lu nuparris* (*nuparris*)

The situation in the last chart is complicated. On the one hand, the prefixed (and in the case of the Assyrian 3rd ps. f. sg. and 1st c. pl. even independent) particle *l(u)-* can be compared to the asseverative *lū* in stative constructions such as *lū balṭāta* 'may you live' (cf. von Soden 1995: 131 = § 81b) and Testen 1993: 1). On the other hand, Huehnergard (1983: 587f.) argues convincingly that the assumption of *lū* as the underlying representation of the prefix in the precative paradigm fails on both

7 The G- and the D-stems are chosen here in order to give a complete overview of the possible contractions of **l(v)-* + preterite form.

orthographical and phonological grounds. According to Huehnergard (1983: 573), it is not even possible to decide whether *lū* preceded *law* in the history of Semitic, or *vice versa*. Huehnergard (1983: 592f.) summarises the situation with good arguments to the effect that, in spite of commonalities, the Semitic particle *lū* / *law* cannot be equated historically with the asseverative prefix *l-* (**la-*) as found in the Akkadian precative paradigm or in Arabic *li-yaqtul* and *fa-l-yaqtul* '(and) let him kill'. Proposals in that direction had been made by Reckendorf (1898: 692 (= § 229)), Brockelmann (1913: 182 (= § 104c), n. 1) – the latter indicating Paul Haupt as his source, and Diakonoff (1965: 82, n. 1). However, one finds clear examples of asseverative *lū* in Akkadian, and this circumstance admittedly complicates the argumentation (as the common origin argument could be strengthened again):

(16) *lū anaddi-kum* 'I will certainly give you'

The status of an asseverative Hebrew particle *lū* (let alone of corresponding Aramaic particles) is uncertain (cf. Huehnergard 1983: 571 in reaction to Nötscher 1953). A possible candidate in our context is the following:

(17) *lū yiśṭəmē-nū yōsēp̄* '(Gen 50:15) 'sure Joseph will despise us'

What suffices for our purposes here is that *lū* / *law* basically serves "to mark a statement as hypothetical, that is, as contrary to fact or to expectation" and "both to introduce unreal conditional sentences and concessive clauses, and to express unattainable wishes" (Huehnergard 1983: 592).[8] There is no point in trying to determine, which function of *lū* / *law* was the "original one". At any rate, it is probably no coincidence that both *lū* / *law* and *l-* (**la-*) contain an *l*-element, even though they cannot be totally equated etymologically.

5 Elliptic conditional clauses as polite injunctions and oath clauses

By now I hope to have established that (a) injunctives and protases may have a comparable distribution, that (b) elliptic conditional clauses are typologically nothing unusual, and that (c) conditional markers are – at

8 In this context, Huehnergard (1983: 593) rejects Reckendorf's (1898: 692 (= §229)) proposal to derive Arabic *law* from *la-wa*.

least in the Semitic scenario – etymologically related to certain injunctive markers. As a result, we are prepared to analyse the two most relevant types of elliptic clauses in our context. In terms of deontic modality, conditional clauses without an apodosis can constitute a formal and polite order or rather injunction. Alternatively, the elliptic conditional clauses can constitute assertory or promissory oath clauses, depending on the use of tense and/or aspect (see below section 6). Let us turn first to the polite order or injunction type. Conditional clauses as polite injunctives (both with the real particle *ʾin* and the irreal particle *law*) are widely attested in Arabic (as they are in many other languages).[9] An example involving the particle *ʾin* is the following:

(18) *fa-ʾin raʾā l-ʾamīru ʾan yaʾmura bi-ʾiṯbāti-hā la-hū*
'if the Emir wishes to order that they [2500 dirham which are the subject of this episode] be ascribed to him' =
'may the Emir be so kind as to order that they be ascribed to him'

Regarding the latter example, Diem (2002: 136) provides a slightly different interpretation: "Wenn also der Emir befehlen möchte, sie [2500 Dirham] ihm gutzuschreiben, (dann möge er es tun!)." Examples involving the Arabic particle *law*, on which I have been focusing so far, include:

(19) *law ʾarsalta ʾilā ṭabībin* 'if you could have sent a doctor' (cf. Brockelmann 1913: 658 (= § 443): 'wenn du doch nach einem Arzt schicken wolltest'))

(20) *law kāna yanfaʿu l-ʾinẓāru* 'if only the postponement would be useful' (cf. Reckendorf 1898: 709 (= § 233)): 'Wenn doch der Aufschub nützte!'

(21) *law rağaʿnā* 'if we returned' = 'let us return'
(cf. Reckendorf 1921: 516: "wie wäre es, wenn wir zurückkehrten")

(22) *law ʾan-nī ʾaʿrifu-hū* 'if I only knew him'

(23) *law saʾalta-hū ʾan yuqīma ʿinda-nā*
'had you only asked him to stay with us'

9 Cf. also Ullmann 1998: 36f. and 53ff.

(24) *ʾinna ʾabā bakrin rağulun raqīqun lā yusmiʿu n-nāsa fa-law ʾamarta ʿumara*
ʻʾAbū Bakr is a weak man whose voice would be difficult for the people to hear, so I wish you ordered ʿUmar [to conduct the prayer].ʼ (cf. Peled 1992: 53)

Comparable examples involving the conditional marker *ʾim* (which is etymologically related with both Akkadian *šumma* and Arabic *ʾin*)[10] are also found in Biblical Hebrew:

(25) *ʾim tittēn ʿērāḇōn ʿaḏ šolḥe-ḵā* ʻcould you give me a collateral until you send outʼ (Gen 38:17) (cf. Brockelmann 1913: 658 (= § 445): ʻwenn du mir ein Pfand gäbest, bis du schickstʼ)

The same observations hold for the conditional marker *lū*:

(26) *lū yišmāʾēl yiḥye lə-p̄āne-ḵā* ʻif only Ishmael could live before youʼ (Gen 17:18) (cf. Brockelmann 1956: 6 (= § 8b): ʻwenn Ismael doch vor dir leben könnteʼ)

In Gəʿəz, one also finds relevant examples involving the particles *sōba* and *ʾəm*:

(27) *sōba mōtna* ʻhad we only diedʼ (cf. Brockelmann 1913: 658 (= § 443))

(28) *ʾəm nassāḥku* ʻif (only) I had repented!ʼ (cf. Lipiński 2001: 547)

Huehnergard (1983: 570), based on Wagner (1953: 19 (= § 24)), also adduces a relevant example from the modern South Arabian language Jibbali (or "Śḥeri"):

(29) *bu-lú yəkīn ʿáśri* ʻwould that he were my husbandʼ

Comparable Akkadian examples involving the particle *lū* exhibit a wider semantic range (cf. Huehnergard 1983: 572 and 2005: 326). I do not consider here concessive clauses (e.g., *kussī-šu lū iḫḫaser* ʻeven though his saddle was brokenʼ) and alternatives in a string of clauses (e.g., *šumma*

10 The same phonological variation is attested in the Semitic causative prefixes (cf. Lipiński 2001: 547f.).

awīlum lū kaspam lū ḫurāṣam lū wardam lū amtam ... ū lū mimma šumšu ... ištām 'if a man has purchased (be it) silver, (be it) gold, (be it) a male slave, (be it) a female slave ... or anything at all ...' = Codex Hammurabi, § 7), which are not directly germane to the discussion at hand. Relevant examples, however, are:

1. optative:

(30) *lū ašpur-aš-šum* "would that I had written him" =
'I should have written him' = 'had I only written him'

(31) *lū awīlat* "would that you were a man" = '(may you) be a man'
(cf. von Soden 1995: 292 (= § 185b) and Huehnergard 1983: 572–574)

2. attainable wishes and injunctions:

(32) *sîn ... lū rābiṣ lemutti-šu* 'may Sîn be the bringer of evil against him'

(33) *lū ṣalmāta lū balṭāta* '(may you) be well and healthy'

3. asseverative particle in oaths (before preterite and durative):

(34) *lū išām* 'indeed he [will have] purchased'

(35) *lū anaddi-kum* 'I will certainly give you'

Let us turn now to the other type of elliptic conditional clauses, namely the so-called oath clauses. There is a clear semantic connection between the oath clauses in Classical Arabic and *šumma (lā)* clauses in Akkadian contractual documents (and elsewhere). In both cases, one can reasonably argue that grammaticalisation has taken place. The "missing" apodosis is no longer felt as such. Grammaticalised *ʾin* / *ʾil-lā* oath clauses are widespread in Classical Arabic. Here are relevant examples:

(36) *ʾanšudu llāha ʿabdan ʿalima ʾanna l-ī tawbatan ʾil-lā ʾaḫbara-nī*
'I implore – by God – a man, who knows my repentence, to tell me' (cf. Brockelmann 1913: 657 (= § 443): 'ich beschwöre bei Gott einen Menschen, der meine Buße kennt, mir zu sagen')

(37) *bi-ḥayāt-ī ʾil-lā ʾanšadta-nī l-bayta*
'by my life, you must recite this verse for me'

(38) *našadtu-ka llāha ʾin rimta hāḏā l-makāna ʾabadan*
'I implore you to never leave this place'

(39) *ʾaqsamtu ʿalay-kum ʾin baraḥtum*
'I implore you not to go away' (cf. Nöldeke 1897: 114)

(40) *ʾaqsamtu ʿalay-ka ʾil-lā ḫaṭabta Lubnā li-bni-ka Qays*
'I implore you to marry Lubnā with your son Qays.'

Wright (1967, vol. 2: 339f. (= § 186, Rem. c)) and Fischer (2006: 205f. (= § 456)), among others, devote some space to this kind of logically inverted oath clauses. The idea is that the negative consequence (apodosis) of the protasis (e.g., *ʾil-lā ḫaṭabta Lubnā li-bni-ka Qays* in the last example) is not mentioned, but nevertheless implied. Therefore, a translation à la "I implore you ..." is warranted in such cases.

Comparable examples are found in both Akkadian (item (41)) and Hebrew (item (42)) (cf. Brockelmann 1913: 658 (= § 445)), and, according to Lipiński (2001: 549), even in Tamazight Berber (item (43)):[11]

(41) *šumma lā iqbi-an-ni*
'if he didn't tell me [that], [may I die]' = "he must tell me"

(42) *ʾim lō(ʾ) neḥzaq mē-hem* 'if we shall not be stronger than they, [may I die] = "we must be stronger than them"

(43) *uḷḷah mš žriḫ* 'by God, if I have thrown [it], [may I die]'

A number of Hebrew oath clauses compiled by Brockelmann (1913: 658f. (= § 445) and 1956: 161f. (= § 170))) illustrate the phenomenon of logical conversion after the particle *ʾim* even better:

(44) *təhī nā ʾālā bēnōṯē-nū ... ʾim taʿăśē ʿimmā-nū rāʿā* (Gen 26:28–29)
'an oath shall be between us ... that you don't do evil to us'
('ein Schwur soll zwischen uns sein, daß du uns nichts Böses tun wirst')

(45) *wə-ḥē napše-ḵā ʾim ʾeʿśe ʾeṯ-had-dāḇār haz-ze* (2 Sam 11:11)
'and as your soul lives, I will not do this thing'
(cf. GKC 472 = § 149c)

11 Examples (41) – (43) are excerpted from Lipiński 2001: 549.

(46) *hinə-nī nišbaʿtī bi-šm-ī hag-gāḏōl ʾāmar YHWH ʾim yihye ʿōḏ šəmī niqrā(ʾ) bə-pī kol ʾīš yəhūḏā ʾōmēr ḥay ʾăḏōn-āy YHWH bə-ḵol ʾereṣ miṣrāyim* (Jer 44:26)
'I hereby swear by my great name, says YHWH – my name shall no more be invoked in the mouth of every Judahite in the land of Egypt who says "(by) the Lord YHWH's life"' (cf. Waltke & O'Connor 1990: 679 = § 40.2.2b)

Again, the (negative) apodoses to the protases *ʾim taʿăśē ʿimmā-nū rāʿā*, *ʾim ʾeʿśe ʾeṯ-had-dāḇār haz-ze*, and *ʾim yihye ʿōḏ šəmī niqrā(ʾ) bə-pī kol ʾīš yəhūḏā* ... are omitted in these examples, thus yielding the inverted logical meaning.

Let it also be mentioned that concessive *kī ʾim* clauses may have their origin in such elliptic constructions, as claimed by Brockelmann (1913: 659 (= § 445c) and 1956: 162 (= § 170c)).[12] An example is the following:

(47) *ḥē p̄arʿō(h) ʾim-tēṣəʾū miz-ze kī ʾim bə-ḇō(ʾ) ʾăḥī-ḵem haq-qāṭan hēnnā* (Gen 42:15) 'by the life of Pharaoh, you shall not get away from here, except if your younger brother comes here' ('beim Leben Pharaos, ihr sollt nicht von hier fortkommen, es sei denn euer jüngerer Bruder komme hierher')

6 *šumma (lā)* clauses in Akkadian treaties

As was stated initially, the phenomenon of (seemingly) elliptic conditional clauses is already attested in Akkadian and analysed as such in Wolfram von Soden's *Grundriß* (1995: 293 (=§ 185g–i)) and John Huehnergard's *Grammar* (2005: 438 (= § 36.3)). Clauses in contracts and treaties beginning with *šumma* 'if' have can be translated by "may you not" and clauses beginning with *šumma lā* can be translated by "may you". (This is not to say that *all* contractual clauses have to start out in this way.) Formally, one could argue that the apodosis is introduced later in the treaty, when the dire consequences are listed, which obtain in the case that the contracting parties do not follow up on the individual clauses. Streck (1998), however, argues against this view.

The Vassal Treaties of Esarhaddon with various Iranian notables are an important case in point (cf. Wiseman 1958 for the *editio princeps* as well as Reiner 1969: 534–541, Borger 1961, 1964; 1983: 160–176, Watanabe

12 On the issue of concessive clauses in this context, cf. also Huehnergard 1983: 574.

1987, and Parpola & Watanabe 1988 for further editions and translations). Streck (1998: 187–190) has analysed the syntactic function of the *šumma (lā)* clauses in this context. Referring to previous work, *inter alia* by Watanabe (1987: 28ff.) and Parpola & Watanabe (1988), he comes to the conclusion that genuine conditional clauses in this textual genre have either a perfect predicate (e.g., § 7, l. 83–84: *šumma [...] ana šīmti ittalak* 'if [...] he has died ...') or a stative (verbal adjective) predicate (e.g., § 12, l. 138–139: *šumma [...] ṣabāti-šunu duāki-šunu maṣâkunu* ... 'if you can arrest (and) kill them ...'). Grammaticalised *šumma (lā)* clauses (a term not used by Streck), however, are always characterised by a predicate in the imperfect (durative), typically in the subjunctive ("affirmative") (e.g., § 4, l. 55: *šumma attunu tunakkarā-šu-ni* '(by God), you will not be hostile to him') and have to be considered syntactically independent in a synchronic perspective.[13] While it is true that promissory oaths are usually expressed by a predicate in the durative (imperfect), the perfect can also occur in such structures, as in item (3) cited above: *šumma ... lā attalk-ak-kim-ma u ṣibût-ki lā ētepuš* 'I will certainly come to you and carry out your wish' (cf. von Soden 1995: 293 (= § 185g).

In the large volume *Ancient Near Eastern Texts Relating to the Old Testament,* Erica Reiner (1969) concedes this grammatical point ("oath clauses") but chooses nevertheless to translate the individual paragraphs with conditional clauses introduced by "if (not)", as do Borger (1983) and Watanabe (1987) in their German translations, but not Wiseman and Parpola & Watanabe in their editions of 1958 and 1988, respectively. In order to illustrate this central issue, the translations of both Reiner (1969), followed by Borger 1983, and Wiseman (1958), followed by Parpola & Watanabe 1988, will be reproduced in the following excerpts of the treaty (following the transcription in Watanabe 1987: 146, 156, and 162). Here comes the first set of provisions in the treaty, which is embedded in paragraph 4:[14]

13 Cf. Streck 1998: 190: "Daher [...] sind sind die Stipulationen [i.e., the individual paragraphs of the treaty, LE] und die Flüche nicht als Protasen und Apodosen eines Konditionalgefüges, sondern als syntaktisch selbständig und die Stipulationen als Schwüre aufzufassen." Cf. also D.O. Edzard 1973 on the question of "moods" in Akkadian in relation to the concept of "subordination".

14 The paragraph numbering is, of course, a modern editorial convention. Still, as in this item, a paragraph may comprise several provisions. Otherwise, both the transcription and the translations are oriented at the line structure in the original tablets (often they cannot made to be totally overlapping).

(48) Vassal Treaties of Esarhaddon, example of several grammaticalised injunctive protases

49 *<šumma attunu> ina eqli ina berti āli*[15]
50 *lā tanaṣṣarā-šū-ni ina muḫḫi-šu lā tamaḫḫaṣā-ni*
51 *lā tamuttā-ni ina ketti ša libbī-kunu*
52 *issē-šu lā tadabbubā-ni milku danqu*
53 *ša gammurti libbī-kunu lā tamallikā-šu-ni*
54 *ḫarrānu danqu ina šēpē-šu lā tašakkanā-ni*
55 *šumma attunu tunakkarā-šu-ni issu libbi aḫḫī-šu*
56 *rabûti ṣaḫ(e)rūti ina kūmu-šu ina kussî Aššur*
57 *tušeššabā-ni šumma abutu ša Aššur-aḫu-iddina šar māt Aššur*
58 *tennânī tušannâ-ni šumma Aššur-bāni-apli mar'a rabi'u*
59 *ša bēt ridūti ša Aššur-aḫu-iddina šar māt Aššur (bēl-kunu)*
60 *(ukallimū-ka-nūni) ḫanûmma lā tadaggalā-ni*
61 *šarruttu bēluttu ša māt Aššur ina muḫḫi-kunu lā u[pp]ašu-nī*

49 'You will
50 protect him in the country and in town; you will fight,
51 and (even) will die, for him. You will speak
52 with him in the truth of your heart, you will give
53 him sound advice loyally.
54 You will set a fair path at his feet.
55 (You swear) that you will not be hostile to him nor will you
56 seat one of his brothers, older or younger, on the throne of Assyria
57 in stead of him. That the word of Esarhaddon, king of Assyria,
58 you will neither change nor alter. That you will
59 serve only Ashurbanipal, the crown-prince,
60 whom Esarhaddon, king of Assyria, your lord (hereby commends),
61 that he will exercise the kingship and dominion over you.'
(Vassal Treaties of Esarhaddon, § 4, Wiseman 1958: 32, 34)

'If you do not serve him in the open country and in the city, do not fight and even die on his behalf, do not always speak the full truth to him, do not always advise him well in full loyalty, do not smooth his way in every respect;
if you remove him, and seat in his stead one of his brothers, younger or older on the throne of Assyria,

15 *<šumma attunu>* probably has to be supplemented here in the initial lacuna; cf. Watanabe 1987: 61, 146.

if you change or let anyone change the decree of Esarhaddon, king of Assyria,
if you will not be subject to this crown prince designate Ashurbanipal, son of Esarhaddon, king of Assyria, your lord, so that he cannot exercise kingship and lordship over you –'
(Vassal Treaties of Esarhaddon, § 4, Reiner 1969: 545)

After a while, the list of clauses is interrupted by paragraph 25, which restates the "ground rules" of the treaty in the form of an anacoluth (part of § 25). As we will see in a moment, this circumstance lends support to the idea of analysing both the stipulations and the curses of the treaty as (synchronically) independent syntactic units:

(49) Vassal Treaties of Esarhaddon, example of an intervening anacoluth
283 *adê annûte ša Aššur-aḫu-iddina šar māt Aššur*
284 *ina muḫḫi Aššur-bāni-apli mar'i šarri rabi'i ša bēt ridūti*
285 *u aḫḫē-šu mar'ē ummī-šu ša Aššur-bāni-apli mar'i šarri rabi'i*
286 *ša bēt ridūti udanninū-ni issē-kunu*
287 *iškunū-ni tāmītu utammû-ka-nūni*

283 'As for these treaty-provisions which Esarhaddon, king of Assyria,
284 has firmly made with you concerning Ashurbanipal,
285 the crown-prince (and) his brothers, son(s) by the same mother
286 as Ashurbanipal, the crown-prince,
287 he has made you take an oath'
(Vassal Treaties of Esarhaddon, § 25, Wiseman 1958: 50)

'This treaty which Esarhaddon, king of Assyria, has established with you in a binding fashion, under oath, on behalf of the crown prince designate Ashurbanipal and his brothers, sons by the mother of the crown prince designate Ashurbanipal,'
(Vassal Treaties of Esarhaddon, § 25, Reiner 1969: 537)

Finally, paragraphs 35 and 36 of the treaty stipulate that the tablet on which the treaty is written may not be altered in any way, let alone be destroyed. It is only in paragraphs 37 to 106 that the series of dire sanctions set in, should the treaty not be followed. Here are paragraphs 37, 38, and 38A:

(50) Vassal Treaties of Esarhaddon, example of several apodoses (curse formulae)

414 *Aššur šar ilānī mušīm [šīmāti] šīmat lemutti*
415 *lā ṭābti liš[īm-k]unu šabût (older editions: abutu) šēbūtu*
416 *kišid littū[ti a]ji iqīš-kunu*
417 *Mullissu ḫīrtu narāmta-šu amāt pî-šu*
418 *lilammin-ma aji iṣbata abbūt-kun*
419 *Sîn nannar šamê u erṣetim saḫaršubbû*
420 *liḫallip-kunu ina pān(ē) ilānī u šarri e<r>ēb-kunu aji iqbi*
421 *kīma sirrē-me ṣabīti ina ṣērim rupdā*

414 '(if you do,) [may Ashur, king of the] gods who decrees the fates,
415 [decree for you] evil and not good. May he never grant
416 you fatherhood and attainment of old age.
417 [May Ninlil], his beloved wife [evilly interpret the] utterance
418 of his mouth evil, may she not intercede for you.
419 [May Sin], the brightness of heaven and earth, clothe you with
420 [a lep]rosy; [may he forbid you entering into the presence of the gods]
421 [or king (saying): 'Roam the desert] like the wild-ass (and the gazelle.'

(Vassal Treaties of Esarhaddon, §§ 37, 38, and 38A, Wiseman 1958: 60)

'May Ashur, king of the gods, who determines the fates, decree for you an evil, unpropitious fate, and not grant you fatherhood, old age, … ripe old age.
May Ninlil, his beloved wife, induce him to pronounce evil for you and may she not intercede for you.
May Anu, king of the gods, rain upon all your houses disease, exhaustion, *di'u*-disease, sleeplessness, worries, ill health.
May Sin, the luminary of heaven and earth, clothe you in leprosy and (thus) not permit you to enter the presence of god and king; roam the open country as a wild ass or gazelle!'
(Vassal Treaties of Esarhaddon, §§ 37, 38, and 38A, Reiner 1969: 538)

Interestingly, the structure of the treaty allows for both a diachronic and a synchronic analysis of the *šumma (lā)* clauses. From a bird's perspective, the large apodosis in the form of dire sanctions stipulates a diachronic analysis. Thus, *šumma (lā)* can be literally translated as "if (not)", as done by Reiner (1969), Borger (1983), and Watanabe (1987). Read in isolation, and especially in view of the intervening anacoluths (e.g., § 25 cited above), a synchronic analysis is warranted, which parses the (historically) conditional *šumma (lā)* clauses as grammaticalised oath sentences, in line with Parpola & Watanabe's (1988) and Streck's (1998) analysis. Such sentences can be rendered simply by an injunctive form, which reverses the "Boolean" value of the clause, i.e. a sentence starting with *šumma* will be translated as "You will (certainly) not ..." and a sentence starting with *šumma lā* will be translated as "You will (certainly) ...". As we have seen, Wiseman (1958) already exploited this option in his translation, which works out nicely, especially in view of the intervening anacoluths in the treaty body.[16] Needless to say, the curses then have also to be understood as independent syntactic units, not as apodoses.

7 Conclusion

Given the comparative Semitic scenario regarding the particles *lū*/*law* and **l(v)* on the one hand and typological observations on "elliptic" conditional clauses on the other hand, the functioning of the Akkadian *šumma (lā)* oath clauses appears to be perfectly natural and understandable. The explanation of such syntactic constructions was further corroborated by recourse to the evidence of comparable constructions in Classical Arabic with *ʾin*/*ʾil-lā* and *law*/*law lā*, as well as in Biblical Hebrew with *ʾim*/*ʾim lō(ʾ)* and occasionally *lū*. The issue of whether the constructions in question diachronically are truly "elliptic" (a notion, which is problematic in the first place) must remain open. Especially in view of the comparable distribution of independent or paratactic injunctive clauses on the one hand and genuine conditional clauses on the other hand, it is equally possible that these constructions are just traces of originally independent optative clauses. In that perspective, the concept of grammaticalisation would not really be pertinent here.[17]

16 Streck (1998: 190, fn. 46) also adduces the case of the intervening precative form *lipluḫū* 'let them rever' in § 34, l. 396, which supports the syntactic independence of the stipulations and the curses.

17 Rubin (2005) does not include optative/conditional particles in his overview of grammaticalisation phenomena in Semitic.

References

Bergsträsser, Gotthelf. 1918–1929. *Hebräische Grammatik.* Leipzig: J.C. Hinrichs'sche Buchhandlung.

Borger, Rykle. 1961 and 1964. "Zu den Asarhaddon-Verträgen aus Nimrud", *Zeitschrift für Assyriologie* 54 (1961): 173-196 and 56 (1964): 261.

Borger, Rykle. 1983. "Assyrische Staatsverträge", in: Borger and Kaiser (eds.) 1983: 155-177.

Borger, Rykle and Otto Kaiser (eds.) 1983. *Texte aus der Umwelt des Alten Testaments.* I/2. Gütersloh: Gütersloher Verlagshaus Gerd Mohn.

Brockelmann, Carl. 1908–1913. *Grundriss der vergleichenden Grammatik der semitischen Sprachen.* 2 Bände. Berlin: Verlag von Reuther & Reichard.

Brockelmann, Carl. 1956. *Hebräische Syntax.* Neukirchen: Verlag der Buchhandlung des Erziehungsvereins Neukirchen Kreis Moers.

Dévényi, Kinga. 1988. "The treatment of conditional sentences by the mediaeval Arabic grammarians: stability and change in the history of Arabic grammar", *The Arabist: Budapest Studies in Arabic* 1: 11–42.

Dévényi, Kinga. 2007. "Jazaʾ", in: Kees Versteegh et al. (eds.). *Encyclopedia of Arabic Language and Linguistics.* Volume II. Eg–Lan, 477–481. Leiden: E.J. Brill.

Diakonoff, Igor. 1965. *Semitokhamitskie jazyki: opyt klassifikatsii (Semito-Hamitic Languages: Essays in Classification).* Moscow: Nauka.

Diehl, Johannes F. 2004. *Die Fortführung des Imperativs im Biblischen Hebräisch.* Münster: Ugarit-Verlag.

Diem, Werner. 2002. "Nichtsubordinatives modales *ʾan yafʿala.* Ein Beitrag zur Syntax der nachklassischen arabischen Schriftsprache", in: Werner Arnold and Hartmut Bobzin (eds.). "Sprich doch mit deinen Knechten aramäisch, wir verstehen es!" *60 Beiträge zur Semitistik. Festschrift für Otto Jastrow zum 60. Geburtstag,* 113–145. Wiesbaden: Harrassowitz.

Edzard, Dietz Otto. 1973. "Die Modi beim älteren akkadischen Verbum", *Orientalia* 42: 121–141.

Fischer, August. 1948. "Grammatisch schwierige Schwur- und Beschwörungsformeln des Klassischen Arabisch", *Der Islam* 28: 1–105.

Fischer, Wolfdietrich. 2006 (4th ed.). *Grammatik des Klassischen Arabisch.* Wiesbaden: Harrassowitz.

Gätje, Helmut. 1976. "Zur Struktur gestörter Konditionalgefüge im Arabischen", *Oriens* 25–26: 148–186.

GKC = Gesenius 1910 = *Gesenius' Hebrew Grammar as edited by the late E. Kautzsch.* Second English edition revised in accordance with the 28th German edition (1909) by A.E. Cowley. Oxford: Clarendon Press.

Haiman, John. 1983. "Paratactic if-clauses", *Journal of Pragmatics* 7.263–281.

Haiman, John. 1986. "Constraints on the form and meaning of the protasis", in: Traugott et al. (eds.) 1986: 215–227.

Huehnergard, John. 1983. "Asseverative *la and hypothetical *lu/law in Semitic", *Journal of the American Oriental Society* 103/3: 569–593.

Huehnergard, John. 2005 (2nd ed.). *A Grammar of Akkadian*. Winona Lake: Eisenbrauns.

Jacobi, Renate. 1967. "Bedingungssätze mit Verschiebung", *Zeitschrift der Deutschen Morgenländischen Gesellschaft* 117: 78–86.

König, Ekkehard. 1986. "Conditionals, concessive conditionals and concessives", in: Traugott et al. (eds.) 1986: 229–246.

Lawler, John M. 1975. "Elliptical conditionals and/or hyperbolic imperatives: some remarks on the inherent inadequacy of derivations", in: Robin E. Grossman et al. (eds.). *Papers from the Eleventh Regional Meeting of the Chicago Linguistic Society*, 371–382. Chicago: The Chicago Linguistic Society.

Lewin, Bernhard. 1970. "Non-conditional 'if' clauses in Arabic", *Zeitschrift der Deutschen Morgenländischen Gesellschaft* 120: 264–270.

Lipiński, Edward. 2001 (2nd ed.). *Semitic Languages. Outline of a Comparative Grammar*. Leuven: Peeters.

Nöldeke, Theodor. 1897. *Zur Grammatik des classischen Arabisch*. Wien. (= 1963. Darmstadt: Wissenschaftliche Buchgesellschaft).

Nötscher, Friedrich. 1953. "Zum emphatischen Lamed", *Vetus Testamentum* 3: 372–380.

Parpola, Simo and Kazuo Watanabe. 1988. *Neo-Assyrian Treaties and Loyalty Oaths*. Helsinki: Helsinki University Press.

Peled, Yishai. 1987. "Conditional sentences without a conditional particle in Classical Arabic prose", *Zeitschrift für Arabische Linguistik* 16: 31–43.

Peled, Yishai. 1992. *Conditional Structures in Classical Arabic*. Wiesbaden: Harrassowitz.

Pritchard, James B. (ed.) 1969 (3rd ed.). *Ancient Near Eastern Texts Relating to the Old Testament*. Princeton: Princeton University Press.

Reckendorf, Hermann. 1898. *Die syntaktischen Verhältnisse des Arabischen*. Leiden: Brill.

Reckendorf, Hermann. 1921. *Arabische Syntax*. Heidelberg: Carl Winter's Universitätsbuchhandlung.

Reiner, Erica. 1969 "Akkadian treaties from Syria and Assyria", in: Pritchard (ed.) 1969: 531-541.

Rubin, Aaron D. 2005. *Studies in Semitic Grammaticalization*. Winona Lake: Eisenbrauns.

Sībawayhi, *Kitāb* = ʾAbū Bišr ʿAmr ibn ʿUṯmān Sībawayhi, *Kitāb Sībawayhi*. Ed. Hartwig Derenbourg, *Traité de grammaire arabe*. 2 vols. Paris: Imprimerie Nationale, 1881–1889. (= Hildesheim: G. Olms 1970)

Streck, Michael P. 1998. "Die Flüche im Sukzessionsvertrag Asarhaddons", *Zeitschrift für Altorientalische und Biblische Rechtsgeschichte* 4: 165-191.

Testen, David. 1993. "The East Semitic precative paradigm", *Journal of Semitic Studies* 38/1: 1–13.

Tietz, Renate. 1963. *Bedingungssatz und Bedingungsausdruck im Koran.* Doctoral dissertation, Tübingen.

Traugott, Elizabeth C. et al. (eds.). 1986. *On Conditionals.* Cambridge: Cambridge University Press.

Trumpp, Ernst. 1881. *Der Bedingungssatz im Arabischen.* Sitzungsberichte der Königlich Bayerischen Akademie der Wissenschaften zu München. Philosophisch-philologische Classe II/4, 337–448. Munich: Verlag der Bayerischen Akademie der Wissenschaften.

Ullmann, Manfred. 1998. *Sätze mit* lau. Munich: Verlag der Bayerischen Akademie der Wissenschaften.

Versteegh, Kees. 1991. "Two conceptions of irreality in Arabic grammar: Ibn Hišām and Ibn Ḥāğib on the particle *law*", *Bulletin d'Études Orientales* 43: 77–89.

Wagner, Ewald. 1953. *Syntax der Mehri-Sprache. Unter Berücksichtigung auch der anderen neusüdarabischen Sprachen.* Berlin: Akademie-Verlag.

Waltke, Bruce and Michael O'Connor. 1990. *An Introduction to Biblical Hebrew Syntax.* Winona Lake: Eisenbrauns.

Watanabe, Kazuo, 1987. *Die* adê-*Vereidigung anläßlich der Thronfolgeregelung Asarhaddons.* Berlin: Gebr. Mann Verlag (Baghdader Mitteilungen, Beiheft 3).

Wiseman, Donald J. 1958. *The Vassal-Treaties of Esarhaddon.* London: The British School of Archeology in Iraq.

Wright, William. 1967 (3rd ed.). *A Grammar of the Arabic Language.* Translated from the German of Caspari, rev. W. Robertson Smith and M. J. de Goeje. 2 vols. Cambridge: Cambridge University Press.

The Interplay of Different Kinds of Commercial Documents at the Red Sea Port al-Quṣayr al-Qadīm (13th c CE)

Andreas Kaplony, Zürich

Abstract

Until recently, documentary evidence on Red Sea shipment consisted mainly of Judaeo-Arabic Geniza documents. This situation has changed with the publication of the Arabic Quṣayr Letters in 2004. Taking these two corpora into consideration and adding another thirty, mostly unpublished Arabic documents, we will try to trace how merchants used a wide range of writings to ensure that their goods arrived safely.

1. Introduction

Today we can hardly imagine how different transportation in earlier times was. To give a few examples: prior to the Digital Revolution of the 1980s, there was no electronic text processing and no e-mail correspondence, while prior to the Industrial Revolution of the nineteenth century, neither mass production of goods nor freight trains existed. But the difference between our digitalized communication *and* mass transportation and that earlier times goes much deeper and also concerns deep-reaching conceptions of how transportation works: Today travelling is supposed to consist mostly of travelling: one leaves home at a given time to arrive at a given time, and in between, one follows a well-defined time schedule. But in pre-modern times – I obviously refer to the Islamic World –, travelling consisted mostly of waiting: upon arriving in a city, one waited for weeks and months for the next caravan to leave. To meet a far-away friend did not mean to agree on an hour, but rather on a week, and if one of them did not arrive the other simply stayed for days until he showed up.

In this paper, I would like to deal not with pre-modern *travel* management, but rather with pre-modern *transportation* management. Nowadays, if a merchant wants to get his goods from one place to another, he sends them in bulks. But in those days, in order to lower the risk of loss merchants not only used to trade in many different merchandises,[1] but

1 For merchants trading in many different merchandises, see Goitein 1967: 153–155; 203 and passim.

also to split their loads and to send them by different carriers; however, in order to keep costs under control, business partners tried to sent consignments to one and the same destination in a joint parcel and considered it worth while doubling or tripling the efforts of organisation.[2] In a world as much used to writing as the Islamic World, all this was reflected in business correspondence, in a sophisticated combination of a whole range of writings. It is the interplay between these writings that is my topic.

2. The Quṣayr Documents and other archives

Until recently, research on the interplay between writings suffered from the peculiar source situation of the about 130,000 Arabic documents preserved from the seventh to the sixteenth century. Most of them were found, since the end of the nineteenth century, by Egyptian peasants and ended up being bought in Cairo by European dealers in antiquities, who brought them to Europe and sold them to the big university libraries of Vienna, Manchester, Prague, etc. Thus, they were well preserved, but due to this long chain of being sold and resold, most carry almost no information *under which circumstances* they were found and *with what documents* they were found *together*.

We have to keep this in mind when we deal with the major archives of Arabic documents known at present. A first type are archives like the Greek, Coptic and Arabic *Qurra b. Sharīk Papyri* (8th c) and the Arabic ninth-century *Marchands d'étoffe Letters* (9th c) both established, *a posteriori*, by scholars browsing collections and identifying groups of similar documents. However, with next to no information on the context, we might only guess if these documents were ever stored together and if so, whose archives these might have been.[3]

---

2 For merchants splitting up their consignments into small parts and putting these together with those of other merchants into new consignments, see Udovitch 1978: 538–539; Meyer 1992: 11; Khalilieh 1998: 98–99; Goitein and Friedman 2007: 164; Margariti 2007: 190; Gil 2008: 253; 265. – To make sure important letters arrived safely, merchants wrote them in a number of copies to be sent by different ships or couriers (Goitein 1954: 185–186; Goitein 1967: 161–162; 284; 288; 304; Almbladth 2004: 22; Goitein and Friedman 2007: 9; Gil 2008: 261). The same procedure was also followed for accounts to be sent (Goitein 1967: 205).

3 The Qurra ibn Sharīk Documents were mainly published in Becker 1908; Bell 1910; for a survey of all editions of the Arabic part, see Diem 1984. The main edition of the Marchands d'étoffe Letters is Rāġib 1982–1996.

A second type are archives of documents most probably stored in one and the same place since centuries, like e.g. the *Khurasan Letters* bought recently as one parcel by the Khalili Collection (8th c; Khan 2007), the *Ḥaram Documents* found in a drawer in the Aqṣà Museum in Jerusalem (13th c; Little 1984), and the archives still to be identified in the centuries-old collections at *Cairo*, on Mount *Sinai*, at *Ardabil*, *Mashhad*, *Palermo*, *Granada*, *Venice*, etc. But the high consistency of these corpora is revealing: they are probably just the core of the respective archive, while other documents were most probably not recognized as having been part of the same archive.[4]

A third type, archives excavated *in situ*, provide a totally different picture: they consist of core-corpora of documents similar to each and a wide range of other documents added: the Greek and Arabic documents from Nessana (4th–8th c), and the Arabic documents from Khirbat al-Mird (7–8th c), al-Quṣayr al-Qadīm (13th c) and Qaṣr Ibrīm (later part, 16–18 c). Most probably, this is also the situation with the corpora that have been excavated and described, but not yet published: the Arabic documents found in Qaṣr Ibrīm (8–10th c), al-Fusṭāṭ and Naqlūn (both 10–11th c), aṭ-Ṭūr (15th–16th c and later), etc.[5]

The *Quṣayr Documents*, mostly fragments, part of the archive of a certain Abū Mufarridj and his son Abū Isḥāq Ibrāhīm, were excavated by the Oriental Institute of Chicago, in 1978, 1980 and 1982, as well as by Southampton University in 1999, 2000, 2001, 2002 and 2003, in the ruins of the former Red Sea harbour al-Quṣayr al-Qadīm.[6] Those from the

4 The Khurasan Letters were published in Khan 2007. Catalogue of the Ḥaram Documents: Little 1984.

5 Editions of the Nessana Documents: Kraemer 1954; of the Khirbat al-Mird Documents: Grohmann 1963; of the later part of the Qaṣr Ibrīm Documents: Hinds and Sakkout 1986; Hinds and Ménage 1991. For the Fusṭāṭ Documents, see Denoix 1986, for the Naqlūn Documents, Kaper 1991; Gaubert 1998; Gaubert and Mouton 2004. – For a survey of Arabic archives preserved, see Grohmann 1954: 7–62; Roemer 1958: 241–244; Bauden 2005; Burke 2007: 211–223; Sijpesteijn 2007. – For the methodological challenge of combining historical texts, documents and archeology for writing the history of al-Quṣayr al-Qadīm, see Burke 2007: 205–223.

6 For the findings at al-Quṣayr al-Qadīm and the general history of the place, see Garcin 1974: 5–6; Whitcomb and Johnson 1979; Whitcomb and Johnson 1982a; Hiebert 1991; Meyer 1992; Peacock and Blue 2006; Burke 2007; Agius 2008: 94–95; 97. – For the papers and inscribed ostrich eggshells found in the Chicago University campaigns, see Dols et al. 1979; Jaeschke 1979: 241; Whitcomb 1979: 39; 52;

three earlier campaigns – the focus of this paper – were found in and outside the so-called Sheikh's House, i.e. the house of the Abū Mufarridj and Abū Isḥāq Ibrāhīm just mentioned. All documents were photographed. A set of these photos is kept at the institute in Chicago, and Donald Whitcomb has been so kind as to share them with us. The original documents found in 1978 were taken to the Ismailiya Museum, those found in 1980 and 1982 to the Cairo Museum of Islamic Arts; some were given to provincial museums. Four documents were published by Gladys Frantz-Murphy, eighty-four more by Li Guo, who additionally used all of them for an in-depth analysis, while another about fifty documents are about to be published by Anne Regourd. In our *Fall 2007 Arabic Papyrology Webclass*, we studied about ten unpublished letters. The following remarks are based on the photos of all documents and are meant to prepare the edition (Kaplony in press) of another twenty documents, both from the 1978 and the 1982 campaigns.

3. Business letters

The most prominent kind of these documents are business letters.[7] There is a clear formulary: (1) The first line has on the right side the *basmala*, on the left side the sender. (2) The second line starts with *al-ladhī uʿlimu bihi* ... "What I would like to make known to [so-and-so, the addressee]" followed by a blessing. (3) The main text is introduced by *wa-siwà dhālika*

57; 59; 64; Frantz-Murphy 1982; Johnson 1982: 264–265; Valentour 1982: 386; 388; Whitcomb and Johnson 1982b: 10; Meyer 1992: 8; Thayer 1993: 203–221; 244–245; Thayer 1995; Guo 1999; Guo 2001; Burke and Whitcomb 2004; Guo 2004 (reviewed by Friedman 2006; Diem 2008a); Burke 2007: 17; 24; 34–36; 38; 40; 42–44; 46–47; 50; 203–315 (with important conclusions drawn from the stratigraphic context the documents were found in); 320–324; 365–387; Margariti 2007: 21–22. – Agius 2008: 18–19; 238. – For the documents found in the Southampton University campaigns, see Regourd 2004; Agius 2005; Agius 2006; Peacock and Blue 2006: 157; 168; 171; 173 (by different authors); Burke 2007: 22–25; Agius 2008: 19–20; Regourd 2008. – All editions of Quṣayr Documents, as well as all later emendations known to us, are included in the *Arabic Papyrology Database* (http://www.ori.uzh.ch/apd), an electronic full-text thesaurus of Arabic papyri and papers.

7 P.Frantz-MurphyQuseir 2; P.QuseirArab. I 1; 2v; 3; 4; 5; 6r; 9; 10; 11; 12; 13; 14r; 15; 16; 18; 19; 20r; 20v [?]; 21; 22; 23r, 24; 25; 31r=II 14b; I 26; 27; 28; 29; 30?; 31v; 32; 33?; 35; 37; 45?; 47; 78; 79; II 1–7; 23; Regourd 2004: 280, fig. 4; possibly also P.QuseirArab. II 8–9.

"and apart from that". (4) For conclusion, there is usually a long list of greetings and a final *wa-s-salām* "and greeting".[8]

The whole letter is interspersed, at pre-defined places, with blessings extended to the addressee. All this obviously follows sophisticated rules by which the sender describes his relationship with the addressee as he, the sender, wants to see it, as part of a much wider *social framework* of common relatives and friends. Why does this re-enacting of a *social framework* through formulas, blessings and greetings take up so much space – about one third, if not more – of each letter? I guess that its main aim was to *re-assure* sender and addressee of their relationship. Long-distance business was based on what Goitein called "formal friendship" and "informal cooperation", i.e. the mutual trust of merchants who used to sell and buy almost autonomously in each other's name or in the name of a joint partnership.[9] This implied that where the sender mentions his wishes, *nota bene*: concerning his own affairs, he necessarily apologises in formulae like *lā taḥtādju waṣīyatan* "... but you obviously do not need any advice", i.e. "please, do not understand my wishes as a sign of mistrust"!

But in between these trust-keeping remarks we do find bits and pieces of *information*.[10] Some of this information is *sensitive and quite explicit*: the sender informs the addressee that he, the sender, has committed, to a certain carrier, a certain consignment, consisting of small numbers of units of a certain kind of goods.[11] By announcing the arrival of the consignment, he allows the addressee to make preliminary arran-

8 For the Quṣayr business letters and their formulary, see Guo 2004: 101–102; 116-121; Regourd 2004: 279–280; Burke 2007: 227. - For Arabic letters, see the surveys by Almbladth 2004; Diem 2008b; Khan 2008; Grob in press.

9 For formal friendship and informal cooperation, see Goitein 1967: 11; 47–48; 164-169; 184–186; Goitein 1971; Udovitch 1977; Margariti 2007: 155–158.

10 Actually, merchants had no interest in just buying and selling. The crucial point was to *know* where to buy and sell which kinds of goods at what price. Thus, their main capital consisted not in goods, but in information, i.e. "the greatest concern of the writers of the Geniza letters was business intelligence" (Goitein 1967: 200–201; see also Udovitch 1978: 527–530).

11 Khalilieh 1998: 95–96. – The small number of units, again, shows the splitting of the bulk of goods and the use of many carriers, as mentioned above. – For a survey of commodities transported in the Red Sea trade and related prices, see Morten 1989: 302–334.

gements. At the latest when the ships were spotted out,[12] he had to be ready to claim his goods from the carrier. With commodities arriving by sea, he had to unload them from the ship[13] and to bring them to his own storing-rooms. With commodities arriving on land, he had to get the loaded pack-animals from the respective caravanserail to his own place. In the case of loss, a letter might have served as piece of evidence that the sender had sent off the goods, an evidence which most probably had to be corroborated by other means. And most important, he had to arrange for transportation further: for consignments brought from the Nile Valley, he had to come to terms with the manager (see part 4 below) of a Red Sea ship to transport them to their destination and to store them at a good place (*mawḍiʿ djayyid*) safe from water, etc.[14] For consignments arriving by sea, he had to send somebody to get pack-animals from Qūṣ in the Nile Valley, as al-Quṣayr was just a small port in the middle of the desert, just an outpost dependent on Qūṣ for food, fodder and fuel supply, a place whereto even water had to be brought from a day's distance,[15] with pack-animals available only accidentally.[16] Matters were, however, slightly different when the merchants at al-Quṣayr waited, in

12 For the importance of spotting out (*tabṣīr*) ships from afar to give the merchants time to make their arrangements, see Goitein 1967: 319–320; Udovitch 1978: 542; Ducatez 2003: 147–148; Margariti 2007: 71; 82; 90; 115–117; 173; Agius 2008: 217; Gil 2008: 273–274.

13 Unloading (and loading) was the merchant's affair, not the carrier's, unless stated otherwise in the transportation contract (Khalilieh 1998: 80–82).

14 To store the goods in a good place (*mawḍiʿ djayyid*) does not refer to a storing-room (as suggested by Burke 2007: XIV; 28; 317), but rather to a place protected from seawater, from falling into the Nile, etc., on a ship. – Burke 2007: 226 assumes that the notes of consignments ("shipping manifests", in her terminology) mostly refer to traffic arriving from the Nile Valley to the Red Sea shore.

15 Whitcomb and Johnson 1979b: 7; Whitcomb and Johnson 1982b: 4; 11–13; Meyer 1992: 2; Burke 2007: 10; 182–183; 297; 322; 326. - Abū Mufarridj himself originated from Qifṭ, see the address P.QuseirArab. I 16v. upside down top down 1-2 *ilà sāḥili l-quṣayri shūnati sh-shaykhi abī mufarridjini l-qifṭīyi* (Guo 2004: 11; 84). Another Qifṭī: *muḥammad al-qayyid al-qifṭī* (Regourd 2004: 280).

16 Murray 1925: 139; 145; Whitcomb and Johnson 1982b; Meyer 1992: 62; 70. Although all these authors refer to Roman time Quṣayr, we might assume that the setting of Muslim Quṣayr was basically the same. However, the merchants of Roman time Quṣayr, and only them, had an uninterrupted chain of watchtowers at their disposal, possibly to send signals to Qūṣ.

spring and in fall, for the mansoon ships coming from India, and for Mecca pilgrims.[17]

What was especially sensitive was all information on *coins sent*,[18] and these are also well-described in number[19] and kind.[20] Coins had to be claimed from the carrier, and in the case of loss, a letter could serve as evidence that the coins had been sent off. But there is more: the fact that coins are mentioned almost as frequently as goods shows the constant lack of ready cash.[21] This was probably one of the problems inherent in a cashless accounting network which consisted of two-person relationships only: merchants did not get their ready cash from one central clearing account into which they were also able to put it back, but had to rely on each other. Despite the existence of a cashless accounting system, business partners did not let their debts grow but were eager to clear their accounts by constantly sending small sums of ready cash.

Other pieces of information were *less sensitive*. Many of those allusions to personal matters, natural disasters or being stuck on the way are probably enigmatic not only to us, but were also not explicit enough to be understood by the recipient, and we should consider the possibility that these allusions were rather key-words to remind the *courier* to provide the addressee with all further details. As we know from Geniza let-

---

17 For the seasonal character of life in al-Quṣayr, see Meyer 1982: 212–213; Wattenmaker 1982: 350; see also Margariti 2007: 38–41.

18 One of the Geniza documents, a note containing information on prices, is even written in mirror script what shows that is was meant to be handled confidentially (Goitein 1967: 218). – For dangers going with sending coins and other especially valuable items, on entrusting those items to the captain personally, and for hiding them inside less valuable consignments, see Goitein 1967: 337; Gil 2008: 257; 275–276. See also a merchant who, at the end of his Arabic list of items sent, writes in Hebrew about coins hidden (Gil 2008: 276). – Sending coins was sensitive not only because of theft, but also because of custom inspection at the arrival. However, neither theft nor custom inspection are mentioned in the Quṣayr Documents. For custom inspection at the arrival, see the remarks on cargo lists (in part 5 below). – For other state control of letters sent, see Goitein 1967: 271–272. – On silk sent in the India trade, instead of coins sent in the Mediterranean, see Goitein 1967: 222.

19 Because of the risk of loss, numbers of coins were also small.

20 Generally on coins mentioned in documents, see Bates 1991.

21 For the general inclination of the time to have one's money work and the consequent lack of cash money, see Goitein 1967: 252–253; 258–259; Margariti 2007: 121; Gil 2008: 275.

ters, letters used to be carried either by acquaintances, friends, relatives and business partners of the sender, or by commercial postal services. But regardless of who the couriers were, they used to carry their letters from house to house and thus in many cases were in a position to complete the letters by word of mouth.[22] However, some letters lengthily report the complications the sender had experienced (P.QuseirArab. I 29) – obviously details not to be explained by the courier.[23]

The *address* of two or three lines on the back of the letter was aimed at this very courier. Its first element is the destination: *yaṣil hādhihi r-ruqʿatu ilà* ... (or in a more refined style: *yaṣil hādhihi l-aḥrufu ilà*) "This note (these letters) are to arrive at [this-and-that place]", i.e. *ilà l-quṣayri* "to [the city of] al-Quṣayr", *ilà sāḥili l-quṣayri* "to the harbour[24] of al-Quṣayr", *ilà shūnati abū mufarridjin* "to the Warehouse of Abū Mufarridj" or even *ilà sāḥili l-quṣayri ilà shūnati abū mufarridjin* "to the harbour of al-Quṣayr, to the Warehouse of Abū Mufarridj". The term *ilà shūnati abū mufarridjin*, if standing alone, obviously was explicit enough for a carrier who, in his post bag, sorted the letters by destination. And: *ilà shūnati abū mufarridjin* refers to a physical *place*, not to the addressee who is named separately.[25]

The name of this *addressee* is the second element of the address: *yusallam li-* ... "To be handed over to [so-and-so]", possibly enlarged by a further characterisation and/or a blessing. Because letters carried sensi-

---

22 For the commercial overland postal service, see Goitein 1964; Goitein 1967: 281–295.

23 For calamities in the high sea, see, e.g., Goitein 1967: 273–352, especially 327-332; Khalilieh 1998: 67–75; 87–105; 155–159; Chakravarti 2002: 49–50; Goitein and Friedman 2007: 157–164; Margariti 2007: 163–175; 199–203; Agius 2008: 216–218; 227–244; Gil 2008: 250–251; 259-264; 264–271.

24 For *sāḥil*, literally "shore", but in this context rather "harbour", see Diem 1991: 262; Friedman 2006: 402; Gil 2008: 280 und 281.

25 The stratification of the documents clearly show that Abū Mufarridj and his son Ibrāhīm had two different firms, even if some letters to Ibrāhīm probably were addressed to Abū Mufarridj (Burke and Whitcomb 2004: 87). Burke 2007: 27–30 and *passim* calls *shūnāt* or shunas the storerooms that are part of the Sheikh's House and each measure between 4 x 2 m and 4 x 5 m (Burke 2007: 28–29; 317). The documents, however, never use the plural, only the singular *shūna*, mostly followed by a personal name. We best assume that *shūna* "warehouse" did not refer just to a single storeroom, but rather to a building with a number of storerooms.

tive information, the addressee is always mentioned explicitly. Most probably, the courier had to hand over the letter to nobody but to this person.

The short final greeting *wa-s-salāmu* "and well-being!", the third part of part of the address, was aimed at the courier. The rare statement *balligh tuʾdjar* "Deliver and you will be rewarded [by the addressee]" (P.QuseirArab. II 5v.2; 23v.2; 78v.5 upside down corr. Friedman) possibly refers to a commercial courier – were all other cases paid by the sender or carried for free by friends or business partners?[26]

4. Notes of consignment

Notes of consignment[27] show a different style. These are short technical notes without *basmala*, in an abbreviated style and almost completely (but see P.QuseirArab. II 15) devoid of blessings. They follow their own formulary:[28] (1) They introduce the name of the addressee by a number of different, although synonymous terms, mostly by *yatasallam* ... "Has to receive [so-and-so, the recipient]", but also by *yusallam ilà* ... or *yusallam li-*... "To be handed over to [so-and-so]", *al-musayyaru ilà* "To be sent to [so-and-so]", *al-wāṣilu ilà* ... "To reach [so-and-so]", or *aṣ-ṣādiru li-yadi* ... "To leave for [so-and-so]". These five ways of introducing a note of consignment possibly mirror five different kinds of senders, i.e. five different places of origins – a characteristic feature of archives which usually fall apart in groups of similar documents, similar in their kind of text and/or their origin, plus a number of alone-standing documents.

The second element of these writs is (2) the name of the sender, introduced by *min* ... "from [so-and-so]". Next comes (3) the name of the carrier,[29] mostly *ṣuḥbata* ... "via [so-and-so]", rarely *ʿalà yadi* ... "via [so-

26 For *balligh tuʾdjar* see Goitein 1964: 119–120; Goitein 1967: 283–284; 304. Goitein, however, interprets the formula the other way round, i.e. as aimed to an acquantaince carrying the letter ("Deliver and you will receive reward [namely from God]") and stating that the addressee will not be responsible for the charge.

27 P.QuseirArab. I 31=II 14a; I 39=II 11; I 40=II 18; I 41=II 12; I 42=II 13; I 43=II 19; I 52=II 10; II 15; 17; probably also Regourd 2004: 278, fig. 2; 279, fig. 3 right.

28 For the Quṣayr notes of consignment, see Guo 2004: 18–22; 102–103. – Generally on notes of consignment, see Regourd 2004: 280–284 ("records/notes of business transactions"); Friedman 2006: 403; Burke 2007: 226–227 ("shipping manifests"); Gil 2008: 278–279 ("shipping certificates"; "*rabb sallim* documents").

29 Friedman 2006: 403 emphasizes that these carriers were not employees, but rather business friend who, by delivering goods, performed a collegial service.

and-so]", or by the name of the boat: *min ḥumūlati* ... "from the load of the [boat called so-and-so]". Then follows (4) the consignment, consisting of one, two or three pieces, each carefully described by the number and kind of goods they contain.

P.QuseirArab. I 52=II 10	(1) *yatasallam* + recipient; consignment; (3) *ṣuḥbat* + carrier remarks
P.QuseirArab. I 39=II 11	(1) *yatasallam* + recipient; (2) *min* + sender; (3) *ṣuḥbat* + carrier; (4) consignment
P.QuseirArab. I 41=II 12	(Recto) (1) *yatasallam* + recipient; (2) *min* + sender; (4) consignment; *yusallimhu li-* + final recipient; (Verso) address
P.QuseirArab. I 42=II 13	(1) *yatasallam* + recipient; (2) *min* + sender; (4) consignment; *wa-hiya min ghallat* + original sender
P.QuseirArab. I 31r=II 14a	(1) *yatasallam* + recipient; (2) *min* + sender; (4) consignment; *wa-hiya li-* + final recipient;
	(3) *wa-ṣuḥbata* + carrier; (4) consignment; *wa-l-ʿushratu wa-l-kirāʾu* + additional costs; *wa-hiya min ghallati* + original sender;
	greetings; consignment; greetings; *wa-l-ʿushratu wa-l-kirāʾu* + additional costs
P.QuseirArab. II 15	(1) *yatasallam* + recipient; (3) *ṣuḥbata* + carrier; [(4) consignment];
	(3) *wa-ṣuḥbata* + carrier; [(4) consignment]
P.QuseirArab. II 17	(1) *yatasallam* + recipient; (2) *min* + sender; [(4) consignment];
	(1) *wa-yatasallam ayḍan*; (2) *min* + sender; [(4) consignment]
P.QuseirArab. I 40=II 18	(1) *yusallam ilà* + recipient; (2) *min* + sender; (4) consignment; (3) *min ḥumūlati* + carrier;
	wa-ayḍan; (4) consignment
P.QuseirArab. I 43=I 19	(1) *yusallam ilà* + recipient; (4) consignment; (3) *min ḥumūlati* + carrier;
	(1) *yusallam ilà* + recipient; (4) consignment; (3) *min ḥumūlati* + carrier
P.QuseirArab. I 38	(1) *yatasallam* + recipient
P.QuseirArab. I 48	(1) *yatasallam* + recipient; final greetings
P.QuseirArab. I 53	(1) *yatasallam* + recipient
P.QuseirArab. I 56	(1) *yatasallam* + recipient

Obviously, these documents were meant to *record* the rather sensitive information that a certain *consignment* sent off by a certain *sender* via a certain *carrier* would be handed over to a certain *recipient*. The existence of an address on verso (P.QuseirArab. I 41=II 12) shows that these documents were transported separately and not attached to the goods: each container had the addressee written directly on it, as some letters explicitly say:[30]

P.QuseirArab. I 14r.3-4[31]	*tusallim lahu l-marīnatayni z-zayti l-ladhī maktūbun ʿalayhim sābiquni l-badrīyu*
	"Hand over to him the two *marīnas* of oil on which is written 'Sābiq al-Badrī'."
P.QuseirArab. I 59.2-4	*al-wāṣilu li-sh-shaykhi abū l-ḥamdi sittatu qiṭaʿi daqīqin wa-qiṭʿatayni aruzz ʿalà r-ruzzi maktūbun abū l-qāsimi*
	"To reach the *shaykh* Abū l-Ḥamd are six bundles of fine flour and two bundles of rice. On the rice is written 'Abū l-Qāsim'."
P.QuseirArab. I 57r.2-4	*al-musayyaru ilà sh-shaykhi abī isḥāqa ibrāhīma bni abī mufarridjin ... ḥimlun kattānun maktūbun ʿalayhim li-sh-shaykhi ḍ-ḍiyāʾi abī l-ḥadjdjādji yūsufa r–rayāfarīyi*
	"To be sent to the *shaykh* Abū Isḥāq b. Abū Mufarridj one load of cotton on which is written 'For the shaykh aḍ-Ḍiyāʾ [i.e., Ḍiyāʾ ad-dīn] Abū l-Ḥadjdjādj Yūsuf ar-Rayāfarī'".

The lack of blessings leaves no doubt that notes of consignments were handed over informally. We know from Geniza documents that goods transported usually were take care of by the merchant owning them or one of his business partners. However, if not, consignments were committed to the captain – strictly speaking rather to the ship manager in charge of storing the consignments – to prevent them from water and thieves, and to defend them, in the case of a shipwreck, against all kinds

30 For labels written with red clay (*mughrā*) or indigo directly on the bags, on patches or wooden plates fastened to their tops, on all sides and on protruding parts, or on skins on the ends, mentioning, possibly, the sender, the carrier, the addressee, the final recipient and the sign (*ʿalāma*) of the firm, see Goitein 1967: 81; 332-337; Khalilieh 1998: 79; 114–115; 174 n. 50; Friedman 2006: 405; Margariti 2007: 190; 195; Gil 2008: 276–279. The existence of signs makes one assume that the porters handling these consignments usually were illiterate.

31 Corr. Friedmann 2008: 405.

of robbers.[32] We may assume that during the journey, this ship manager was keeping a separate writ for each consignment and on his arrival at a certain harbour, used this writ to hand over, together with the writ, all relevant containers and to obtain the freight and his wage. The Geniza documents show that the recipient did not necessarily un-pack the goods, but checked their number and kind only superficially.[33]

At the top of two thirds of these writs, and of these writs only, we find an enigmatic sign. This sign mostly consists of a hook and a final *yāʾ*, but in one instance, we find a quite clear, although undotted *baqiya* "has remained". In a variant, we have an undotted *djīm* with an extraordinarily long tail, respectively this long tail only.

hook-*yāʾ* (tail straight to the right)	P.QuseirArab. I 31r=II 14a; II 16; P.Vind.Arab. III 56r; 59r
hook-*yāʾ* (tail sickle-like)	P.QuseirArab. ; I 23r; 24; 25r; 26; 27; 28r; I 39=II 11
hook-*yāʾ* (upper part long and upright)	Guo 2004: p. 113 pl. 3 middle left; P.Vind.inv. A.Ch. 36658v
baqiya (in circle-plus-wavy-line tail)	P.QuseirArab. II 22
hook-hook-*yāʾ* (tail underline-like)	P.QuseirArab. II 21
djīm (with long tail)	P.QuseirArab. II 20r
(long tail only)	P.QuseirArab. I 52=II 10

32 Goitein 1967: 157. – For the role of the manager (*wakīl, sarhang*) of a ship, definitely to be differentiated both from the ship's owner (*ṣāḥib, nākhudā*) after whom it was named, and from its captain (*raʾīs, rayyis, muʿallim*) – in the case of a captain sailing his own ship, the last two terms were interchangeable – and for the storing of the goods by the manager, see Cahen 1964: 235; Goitein 1967: 225; 296–298; 312–314; 337–338; 342 (488) n. 11; Khalilieh 1998: 37; 42; 53–55; 74–75; 79–80; 91–92; 148–149; Chakravarti 2000: 37–39; Ducatez 2003: 148 n. 82; Goitein and Friedman 2007: 121–156; Margariti 2007: 143–150; 220; Gil 2008: 248–249; 265–267; 274–275; Agius 2008: 178–182; see also the difference between the manager (*toicharchos*), the ship owner (*nauklēros, navicularius*), the captain (*kybernētēs, gubernator*) and the first mate (*proreus*) of Greek and Roman-time ships (Casson 1971: 314–321; Meyer 1992: 55), and the crew on board ships sailing the Indian Ocean (Serjeant 1970; Chakravarti 2002: 49–56; Agius 2008: 175–185).

33 For the slow unpacking of goods, see Goitein 1967: 338. Consignments, however, also had to be aired to prevent damage by prolonged exposure to shipboard moisture (Margariti 2007: 189–190).

These signs were added later, as the long tail of P.QuseirArab. I 52=II 10; II 20r written across the main text shows. There has been some discussion on what these signs mean. I am inclined to consider them as personal registration marks by which some recipients marked *a whole document* as being settled.[34] Possibly, they used these writs to keep track of which goods they had in their storehouse – and this would explain why these writs were found in the archive.[35]

But this is not all. One sender added, on the same sheet of paper, a second full note of consignment, mentioning the same recipient and the same carrier (P.QuseirArab. I 43=II 19), another sender added two abbreviated entries, first on a new line: *wa-yatasallam ayḍan min ...* "And he has to receive also from [so-and-so] ...", plus a consignment, and then, again on a new line, *wa-ayḍan* "And also ...", plus a consignment (P.QuseirArab. I 40=II 18). Some writs specify from whom the goods had come, possibly an information on quality: *wa-hiya min ghallati ...* "and this is from the grain of [so-and-so, the very first sender]", while others order that they be forwarded: *wa-hiya li-...* "and it belongs to [so-and-so, the final recipient]" or *yusallimhu li-...* "and he shall hand it over to [so-and-so]". One hybrid document, explicitly called a memorandum (*tadhkira*), starts as a note of consignment, specifies transportation costs and cus-toms paid: *wa-l-ʿushratu arbaʿīna [dīnāran] wa-l-kirāʾu sittatu amdādin* "and the tithe is fourty [*dīnār*] and the rent six *mudd*", repeated later as "*wa-l-kirāʾu sittatu amdādin wa-l-ʿushratu arbaʿīna [dīnāran]* "and

34 Diem 1996: 263 considers this sign a registration mark, Guo 1999: 176; Guo 2004: 111–114 an abbreviated *basmala*. But if this was an abbreviated *basmala,* why does P.QuseirArab. I 22 carry a full *basmala* (Friedman 2008: 406, also mentioned by Guo himself, Guo 2004: 112 n. 26; 189)? Friedman 2008: 405–406 considers this a sign to mark that the text of recto is continued on verso. – These signs clearly refer to the *whole document*. For line-related signs to check and clear *single entries* on a document, see part 6 below. – I owe the reference to P.Vind.inv. A.Ch. 36658v to the kindness of Werner Diem, Cologne.

35 Inside the Sheikh's House, the concentration of documents was especially high in North House, Room C, phase IIb, the one room closely associated with Ibrāhīm b. Abī Mufarridj, while other documents were found in other rooms and covered there with each new application of plaster. Ibrāhīm probably used to keep his business letters for a short time, possibly for use them as scrap papers (Burke 2007: 244; 280; see also Burke and Whitcomb 2004: 87). However, we also could argue that he was keen to keep a choice of letters, while he allowed others to be spread and get lost.

the rent is six mudd and the tithe 40 [dīnār]",[36] and develops into a full letter with a long list of greetings, etc. (P.QuseirArab. II 14a).

5. A process slip

But how would a ship manager prove that he actually *had* delivered some goods? He probably, in his turn, received a *receipt of delivery*, but to find such receipts of delivery, we would need to find a ship manager's archive, not a merchant's archive as the one we have.[37] A ship manager's archive would also have preserved two other types of documents: cargo lists to be presented to the custom authorities upon arrival[38] and departure permits issued by the port authorities,[39] both devices to enable the authorities to force the merchants passing by to sell those goods they (the authorities) were interested in.[40] I have not been able to identify, in the Quṣayr Documents, neither receipts issued for carriers, nor cargo lists, nor permits of departure preserved, but at least the later two are mentioned in Geniza documents.

No receipt of delivery is P.QuseirArab. I 60=Nr. 20, despite the fact that it mentions first the recipient: *alladhī qabaḍa bū mufarridjin* "this is

36 For transportations costs, incl. ship rents, see Goitein 1967: 339–346; Gil 2008: 253; 255; 265; 279–282. – The term *salfa* "payment in advance", i.e. ship rent (Gil 2004: 90; Gil 2008: 279) is unknown to the Quṣayr Documents.

37 Similarly Guo 2004: 47.

38 Terms used for "cargo list" are *sharbīl / sharanbal / sharanbul* (pronunciation unsure), *satmī/shatmī (al-markab/ar-rubbān)* or *ruqʿa* in the Indian Ocean, and *shāmil* in the Mediterranean. – For cargo lists and the inspection of the ship *en route* and upon arrival, see Idris 1961: 236 n. 2 (*sharbīl, sharanbal*); Cahen 1964: 252; 303; Cahen 1978: 309–310; Goitein 1967: 351; Smith 1995: 129–130; Khalilieh 1998: XV; XVIII; 29; 46; 56; 82–87; 93–94; 140; Ducatez 2003: 148–149; Goitein and Friedman 2007: 131 (*sharanbul*); Margariti 2007: 82; 87–88; 110–140; 167–168; 189; 207; Agius 2008: 227–230; 312; Gil 2008: 278. In Ibn al-Mudjāwir's *Mustabṣir* referring to Mamlūk Aden, basic commodities like wheat and flour, the two main commodities of the Quṣayr Documents, are exempt customs dues (Smith 1995: 133; Ducatez 2003: 153; Margariti 2007: 135). The paper work proper was not done by the ship manager himself, but by the ship scribe (*karrānī*).

39 For departure permits (sing. *sarāḥ*) and the inspection of the ship before departure, see Goitein 1967: 59; Gil 2008: 279; Khalilieh 1998: 31–32; 79; 85–87; 145; Khalilieh 2005: 249–250; Margariti 2007: 3–6; Agius 2008: 227–230.

40 On authorities seizing merchandises passing through, see Goitein 1967: 60; Morten 1989: 294; 296; Goitein and Friedman 2007: 124–125; Margariti 2007: 167–168.

what has received Abū Mufarridj" and then the consignment. But the document does not continue with the name of the sender – let us keep in mind that the basic function of a receipt of delivery is to absolve the sender of having handed over a certain consignment to the recipient –, but with the name of the final recipient *li-yūsufa bni barṭūṭa* "[to be handed over] to Yūsuf ibn Barṭūṭ". The document is explicitly labelled *tadhkiratun mubārakatun in shāʾa llāhu* "a memorandum/report, hopefully blessed",[41] and across this title runs the tail of one of our enigmatic signs. This is a *process slip* which most probably had been attached to the consignment in the port, if not earlier, which has been marked as being settled some-time later, but nevertheless was kept in the files of Abū Mufarridj.

If we turn this very document upside-down we find a similar mark, possibly starting with *alladhī qabaḍa ʿīsà* "this is what has received ʿĪsà" followed by the consignment. A short note on verso summarises: *baqiya ʿalà ʿīsà* ... "Remains to be paid by ʿĪsà ..." plus (3) a number of *dirhams*. Obviously, this paper had been used a first time as a process slip for a similar transaction concerning this ʿĪsà, and later a second transaction in favour of Yūsuf ibn Barṭūṭ.

6. Accounting Journals

The last kind of documents to mention in our context are lists which gather all the information about all goods business partners had sent and received. And indeed, some few pages of this kind of accounting journal have been preserved.

In such an accounting journal (*daftar*),[42] each entry starts on a new line and runs across one or two lines, either in two columns or in one. Column titles are missing, but this might be by accident. Each single

---

41 Cf. *bayānun mubārakun* (P.QuseirArab. I 61.1).

42 For accounting journals from Quṣayr, see Guo 2004: 45–46; 104; Regourd 2004: 280, on commercial accounting journals in general, Goitein 1967: 152; 204–209; Khalilieh 1998: 94–95; Margariti 2007: 193; 196. For the impact of Arabic accounting on medieval Western accounting, see Goody 1996: 49–81. – For a similar instance where keeping in mind the *actual place* of an archive is crucial, see Gil 2008: 261 n. 13. Gil convincingly argues that most letters ending up in the Cairo Genizah were written in the West, whereas letters sent from Cairo only exceptionally were stored in Cairo. This was the reason, he argues, why the Geniza documents almost exclusively mention ships sailing, on the Mediterranean, from East to West (*sic*, against Cahen in Udovitch 1978: 553), but not the opposite way.

entry begins with a plain name (*ism*) without any further details, which most probably shows that the number of business partners a merchant used to deal with was fairly small. Next comes one and only one quantity of grain (P.QuseirArab. I 2r; 64, see P.QuseirArab. I 49), of *dirhams* (P.QuseirArab. I 67), or of perfume and spice (P.QuseirArab. I 68). It seems that records for grain, for ready cash, and for perfume and spice were kept separately.[43]

On the two *grain* lists, and only there, the name of the sender and the quantity of grain are followed by *naqṣuhu* "his allowance" and a smaller quantity of grain. This possibly refers to the difference between the quantity of grain announced (as measured before transport) and the one received (as measured after transport), an unavoidable difference due to the fact that by being shaken, grain becomes more compact and thus looses volume.[44] In the *dirham* journal, and only there, lines are crossed out (P.QuseirArab. I 67) what possibly indicates the regular clearance of accounts.[45] This, however, seems to imply that *dirham* accounts did not refer to sums which had arrived, but rather to those sent.

7. Conclusion

A closer look at the recently found archive of two merchants, a certain Abū Mufarridj and his son Abū Isḥāq Ibrāhīm, living in the thirteenth century Red Sea harbour al-Quṣayr al-Qadīm, shows a clear interplay of at least four different kinds of documents: *letters* to announce the arrival

---

43 Similarly, different goods were kept in separate rooms. In the so-called Sheikh's House, wheat was kept in Room E (Burke 2007: 60), textiles in Shunas B and D (Burke 2007: 192).

44 For the regular measuring of goods before and after transport, see Goitein 1967: 339; Thayer 1993: 146–148; 214; Margariti 2007: 119. – Guo 2004: 45–46 rightly stresses that the term *nuqṣa* (should be *naqṣ*) is quite common in the Quṣayr Documents and that it refers to the common re-weighing of grain upon arrival. He, however, interprets *naqṣa* as "shortage" of [non-standard] weights. But why should this have affected grain more than other goods? Frantz-Murphy 1982 points out that the [seeming] loss of grain was much discussed and resulted in the loading and unloading of grain in the presence of witnesses. – Another option would be to understand *naqṣ* as a synonym of *ṭarḥ* "tare, weight of the container", but again, why should this be mentioned for grain only?

45 For the checking and clearing of the single entries of an account and for respective *line-related marks*, see Grohmann 1938: 133; 136; 215; 226; Grohmann 1952: 10–11; 19; 25; 131; 133; 273; Guo 2004: 33; 45; Regourd 2008: 15. For similar signs referring to a whole document, see part 4 above.

of a certain consignment, *notes of consignment* transported by a carrier, *process slips* for instructions how to handle a consignment, and *account journals* to keep track of the consignments that had arrived.

Bibliography

Agius, Dionisius Albertus 2005. " 'Leave Your Homeland in Search of Prosperity': The Ostrich Egg in a Burial Site at Quseir al-Qadim in the Mamluk Period", in: Vermeulen, U[rbain] and van Steenbergen, J[o] (eds.). *Egypt and Syria in the Fatimid, Ayyubid and Mamluk Eras, vol. 4. Proceedings of the 9th and 10 International Colloquium Organized at the Katholieke Universiteit Leuven in May 2000 and May 2001.* Orientalia Lovaniensia Analecta, vol. 140. Leuven: Peeters: 355–379.

Agius, Dionisius 2006. "The Inscribed Ostrich Egg", in: Peacock and Blue 2006: 158–160.

Agius, Dionisius A. 2008. *Classic Ships of Islam: From Mesopotamia to the Indian Ocean.* Handbook of Oriental Studies. Section 1: The Near and Middle East, vol. 92. Leiden: Brill.

Almbladh, Karin 2004. "The Letters of the Jewish Merchant Abū l-Surūr Faraḥ b. Ismā'īl al-Qābisī in the Context of Medieval Arabic Business Correspondence", *Orientalia Suecana* 53: 15–35.

Bates, Michael L. 1991. "Coins and Money in the Arabic Papyri", in: Rāġib, Yūsuf (ed.). *Documents de l'Islam médiéval: nouvelles perspectives de recherche: Actes de la Table Ronde (Paris, 3–5 mars 1988)* ... Publications de l'Institut Français d'Archéologie Orientale, vol. 714. Textes arabes et études islamiques, vol. 29. Cairo: Institut Français d'Archéologie Orientale: 44–64.

Bauden, Frédéric. 2005. "Mamluk Era Documentary Studies: the State of the Art", *Mamluk Studies Review* 9: 15–60.

Becker, C[arl] H. 1906. *Papyri Schott-Reinhardt, vol. I.* Veröffentlichungen aus der Heidelberger Papyrussammlung [VHP], vol. 3. Heidelberg: Winter.

Bell, H[arold] I. 1910. *The Aphrodito Papyri: With an Appendix of Coptic Papyri edited by W.E. Crum.* Greek Papyri in the British Museum: Catalogue, With Texts, vol. 4. London: British Museum.

Burke, Katherine Strange 2007. *Archaeological Texts and Contexts on the Red Sea: the Sheikh's House at Quseir al-Qadim.* PhD thesis University of Chicago; free download from http://oi.uchicago.edu/pdf/ksburke_dissertation.pdf; 9 August 2009.

Burke, Katherine Strange and Whitcomb, Donald 2004. "Quṣeir al-Qadīm in the Thirteenth Century: A Community and its Textiles." *Ars Orientalis* 34 (= Communities and Commodities: Western India and the Indian Ocean, Eleventh/Fifteenth Centuries): 83–97.

Cahen, Claude 1964. "Douanes et commerce dans les ports méditerranéens de l'Egypte médiévale d'après le Minhādj d'al-Makhzūmī", *Journal of the Economic and Social History of the Orient* 7: 217–314.

Cahen, Claude 1978. "Ports et chantiers navales dans le monde méditerranéen jusqu'aux croisades", in: *La navigazione mediterranea nell' alto medioevo: settimane di studio del Centro Italiano di Studi sull' Alto Medioevo XXV, 14–20 aprile 1977*. Spoleto: Studio del Centro Italiano di Studi sull' Alto Medioevo: 299–319.

Casson, L. 1971. *Ships and Seamanship in the Ancient World*. Princeton: Princeton University Press.

Chakravarti, Ranabir 2000. "Nakhudas and Nauvittakas: Ship-owning Merchants in the West Coast of India (c. AD 1000–1500)", *Journal of the Economic and Social History of the Orient* 43: 34–64.

Chakravarti, Ranabir 2002. "Seafaring, Ships and Ship Owners: India and the Indian Ocean (AD 700–1500), in: Parkin, David and Barnes, Ruth (eds.). *Ships and the Maritime Technology in the Indian Ocean*. Indian Ocean Series. London: Curzon: 28–61 (=Chapter 2).

Denoix, Sylvie 1986. "Les ostraca de Isṭabl ʿAntar", *Annales Islamologiques* 22: 27–33; pl. XIII–XV.

Diem, Werner 1984. "Philologisches zu den arabischen Aphrodito-Papyri", *Der Islam* 61: 268–273.

Diem, Werner 2008a. "Besprechung von 'Guo, Li. Commerce, Culture and Community in a Red Sea Port in the Thirteenth Century: The Arabic Documents from Quseir. Islamic History and Civilization. Studies and Texts, vol. 52. Leiden: Brill, 2004'", *Zeitschrift der Deutschen Morgenländischen Gesellschaft* 158: 164–170.

Diem, Werner 2008b. "Arabic Letters in Pre-Modern Times: A Survey with Commented Selected Bibliographies", in: Grob and Kaplony 2008: 885–906.

Diem, Werner and Radenberg, Hans-Peter 1994. *A Dictionary of the Arabic Material of S.D.Goitein's 'A Mediterranean Society'*. Wiesbaden: Harrassowitz.

Dols, Michael et al. 1979. "Arabic Inscriptions", in: Whitcomb and Johnson 1979a: 247–249.

Ducatez, Guy 2003. "Aden et l'Océan indien au XIIIe siècle: navigation et commerce d'après Ibn-al-Muǧāwir", *Annales Islamologiques* 37: 137–156.

Frantz-Murphy, Gladys 1982. "The Red Sea Port of Quseir: Arabic Documents and Narrative Sources", in: Whitcomb and Johnson 1982a: 267–283 (= Chapter 13).

Friedman, Mordechai 2006. "Quṣayr and Geniza Documents on the Indian Ocean Trade", *Journal of the American Oriental Society* 126: 401–409.

Garcin, Jean-Claude 1974. *Un centre musulman de Haute-Egypte médiévale: Qūṣ*. Publications de l'Institut Français d'Archéologie Orientale, vol. 496. Textes arabes et études islamiques, vol. 6. Cairo: Institut Français d'Archéologie Orientale.

Gaubert, Christian 1998. "Naqlun: remarques préliminaires sur les archives d'époque fatimide d'une famille copte", *Polish Archaeology in the Mediterranean* 9: 87–89.

Gaubert, Christian and Mouton, J[ean]-M[ichel] 2004. "Présentation des achives d'une famille copte du Fayoum à l'époque fatimide", in: Immerzeel, M[at] and van der Vliet, J[acques] (eds.). *Coptic Studies on the Threshold of a New Millennium*. Orientalia Lovanensia Analecta, vol. 133. Leuven: Peeters: 505–517.

Gil, Moshe 2004. "The Flax Trade in the Mediterranean in the Eleventh Century A.D. As Seen in Merchants' Letters from the Cairo Genizah", *Journal of Near Eastern Studies* 67: 81–96.

Gil, Moshe 2008. "Shipping in the Mediterranean in the Eleventh Century A.D. as Reflected in Documents from the Cairo Geniza", *Journal of Near Eastern Studies* 67: 247–292.

Goitein, S[hlomo] D. 1954. "From the Mediterranean to India: Documents on the Trade to India, South Arabia, and East Africa from the Eleventh and Twelfth Centuries", *Speculum* 29: 181–197.

Goitein, S[hlomo] D. 1964. "The Commercial Mail Service in Medieval Islam", *Journal of the American Oriental Society* 84: 118–123.

Goitein, S[hlomo] D. 1967. *A Mediterranean Society: The Jewish Communities of the Arab World as Portrayed in the Documents of the Cairo Geniza, Vol. 1: Economic Foundations*. Berkeley; Los Angeles: University of California Press.

Goitein, Shelomo D. 1971. "Formal Friendship in the Medieval Middle East", *Proceedings of the American Philosophical Society* 115: 484–489.

Goitein, S[hlomo] D. and Friedman, Mordechai Akiva 2007. *India Traders of the Middle Ages: Documents From the Cairo Geniza ('India Book')*. Etudes sur le Judaïsme Médiéval, vol. 31. Leiden: Brill.

Goody, Jack 1996. *The East in the West*. Cambridge: Cambridge University Press.

Grob, Eva Mira in press. *Documentary Arabic Private and Business Letters on Papyrus: Form and Function, Content and Context*.

Grob, Eva Mira and Kaplony, Andreas (eds.). *Documentary Letters from the Middle East: The Evidence in Greek, Coptic, South Arabian, Pehlevi, and Arabic (1st–15th c CE)*, Bern: Lang, 2008 = *Asiatische Studien* 62,3: 671–906.

Grohmann, Adolf 1938. *Arabic Papyri in the Egyptian Library, vol. 3: Administrative Texts, With a Contribution by C.Schmidt*. Cairo: Egyptian Library Press.

Grohmann, Adolf 1952. *Arabic Papyri in the Egyptian Library, vol. 4: Administrative Texts*. Cairo: Egyptian Library Press.

Grohmann, Adolf 1954. *Einführung und Chrestomathie zur arabischen Papyruskunde, vol. 1: Einführung*. Monografie Archivu Orientálního, vol. 13,1. Prague: Státní Pedagogické Nakladalství.

Grohmann, Adolf 1963. *Arabic Papyri from Ḫirbet el-Mird*. Bibliothèque du Muséon, vol. 52. Louvain: Publications universitaires, Institut orientaliste.

Guo, Li 1999–2001. "Arabic Documents from the Red Sea Port of Quseir in the Seventh/Thirteenth Century", *Journal of Near Eastern Studies* 58: 161–190; 60: 81–116.

Guo, Li 2004. *Commerce, Culture and Community in a Red Sea Port in the Thirteenth Century: The Arabic Documents from Quseir*. Islamic History and Civilization. Studies and Texts, vol. 52. Leiden: Brill. [P.Quseir I].

Hiebert, Fredrik T. 1991. "Commercial Organization of the Egyptian Port of Quseir al-Qadim: Evidence from the Analysis of the Wooden Objects", *Archéologie islamique* 2: 127–159.

Hinds, Martin and Ménage, Victor 1991. *Qaṣr Ibrīm in the Ottoman Period: Turkish and Further Arabic Documents*. Texts from Excavations, vol. 11. London: Egypt Exploration Society.

Hinds, Martin and Sakkout, Hamdi 1986. *Arabic Documents From the Ottoman Period from Qaṣr Ibrīm*. Texts from Excavations, vol. 8. London: Egypt Exploration Society.

Idris, H[ady] R[oger] 1961. "Commerce maritime et ḳirāḍ en Berbérie orientale d'après un recueil inédit de fatwās médiévales", *Journal of the Economic and Social History of the Orient* 4: 225–239.

Jaeschke, Richard L. 1979 "Conservation", in: Whitcomb and Johnson 1979a: 237–242 (= Chapter 9).

Johnson, Janet H. 1982. "Inscriptional Material", in: Whitcomb and Johnson 1982: 263–266 (= Chapter 12).

Kaper, Olaf E. 1991. "Arabic Papyri and Inscriptions from Naqlun, Hermitage No. 89", *Polish Archaeology in the Mediterranean* 2: 57–59.

Kaplony, Andreas in press. "Zweiundzwanzig Geschäftsbriefe, Geleitscheine, Laufzettel und Geschäftsjournale aus dem Rotmeer-Hafen al-Quṣayr al-Qadīm (13. Jh.)". [P.Quseir II].

Khalilieh, Hassan S. 1998. *Islamic Maritime Law: An Introduction*. Studies in Islamic Law and Society, vol. 5. Leiden: Brill.

Khalilieh, Hassan S. 2005. "Capacity and Regulations Against Overloading of Commercial Ships in Byzantine and Islamic Maritime Practices", *Journal of Medieval History* 31: 243–263

Khan, Geoffrey 2007. *Arabic Documents From Early Islamic Khurasan*. Studies in the Khalili Collection, vol. 5. London: Khalili Collection.

Khan, Geoffrey 2008. "Remarks on the Historical Background and Development of Early Arabic Documentary Formulae", in: Grob and Kaplony 2008: 885–906.

Kraemer, Casper J. Jr. 1958. *Excavations at Nessana, vol. 3: Non Literary Papyri*. Princeton: Princeton University Press.

Little, Donald P. 1984. *A Catalogue of the Islamic Documents from al-Ḥaram aš-Šarīf in Jerusalem*. Beiruter Texte und Studien, vol. 29. Beirut: comm. Steiner.

Margariti, Roxani Eleni 2007. *Aden and the Indian Ocean Trade: 150 Years in the Life of a Medieval Arabian Port*. Islamic Civilization and Muslim Networks. Chapel Hill: University of North Carolina Press, 2007.

Meloy, John 1998. *Mamluk Authority, Meccan Autonomy, and Red Sea Trade, 797–859/1395–1455*. PhD thesis University of Chicago 1998 [not accessible].

Meyer, Carol 1982. "Large and Small Storerooms of the Roman Villa", in: Whitcomb and Johnson 1982: 201–213 (= Chapter 7).

Meyer, Carol 1992. *Glass from Quseir al-Qadim and the Indian Ocean Trade*. Studies in Ancient Oriental Civilization, vol. 53. Chicago: The Oriental Institute of the University of Chicago, 1992.

Morten, Richard T. 1989. "Prices in Mecca During the Mamluk Period", *Journal of the Social and Economic History of the Orient* 32: 279–334.

P.QuseirArab. I see Guo 2004.

P.QuseirArab. II see Kaplony 2010.

Peacock, David and Lucy Blue 2006. *Myos Hormos – Quseir al-Qadim: Roman and Islamic Ports on the Red Sea, vol. 1: Survey and Excavations 1999–2003*. Oxford: Oxbow.

Rāġib, Yūsuf 1982–1996. *Marchands d'étoffes du Fayyoum au IIIe/IXe siècle d'après leurs archives (actes et letters), vol. 1; 2; 3; 5,1*. Suppléments aux Annales Islamologiques: Cahiers, vol. 2; 5; 14; 16. Publications de l'Institut Français d'Archéologie Orientale, vol. 586; 631; 727; 768. Cairo: Institut Français d'Archéologie Orientale.

Regourd, Anne 2004. "Trade on the Red Sea During the Ayyubid and Mamluk Periods: The Quṣeir Paper Manuscript Collection 1999–2002, First Data", *Proceedings of the Seminar for Arabian Studies* 34: 277–292.

Regourd, Anne 2008. "Folding of a Paper Document from Quseir al-Qadim: A Method of Archiving?", *al-ʿUṣūr al-Wusṭà* 20: 13–16.

Roemer, Hans Robert 1958. "Documents et archives de l'Egypte islamique", *Mélanges de l'Institut Dominicain d'Etudes Orientales du Caire* 5: 237–252

Serjeant, R.B. 1970. "Maritime Customary Law Off the Arabian Coasts", in: Mollat, Michel (ed.). *Sociétés et compagnies de commerce en Orient et dans l'Océan Indien: actes du Huitième Colloque international d'histoire maritime (Beyrouth – 5–10 september 1966)*. Bibliothèque générale de l'Ecole pratique des hautes etudes. VIe section, [vol. 8]. Paris: S.E.V.P.E.N.: 195–207.

Sijpesteijn, Petra M. 2007. "Arabic Papyri and Other Documents from Current Excavations in Egypt, With an Appendix of Arabic Papyri and Some Written Objects in Egyptian Collections". *al-Bardiyyat* 2: 10–23; free download from http://www.ori.uzh.ch/isap/isapprojects.html; 5 November 2009.

Smith, Rex 1995, reprint 1997. "Have you Anything to Declare? Maritime Trade and Commerce in Ayyubid Aden: Practices and Taxes, *Proceedings of the Seminar for Arabian Studies* 25: 127–140. Reprint with corrigenda in: Smith, G. Rex, *Studies in the Medieval History of the Yemen and South Arabia*. Variorum Collected Studies Series, vol. CS 574. Aldershot: Variorum, 1997: Paper X; Addenda and corrigenda 3–4.

Smith, Rex 1996, reprint 1997. "More on the Port Practices and Taxes of Medieval Aden", *New Arabian Studies* 3: 208–218. Reprint with corrigenda in: Smith, G. Rex, *Studies in the Medieval History of the Yemen and South Arabia*. Variorum Collected Studies Series, vol. CS 574. Aldershot: Variorum, 1997: Paper XI; Addenda and corrigenda 3.

Thayer, Jennifer Mott 1993. *Land Politics and Power Networks in Mamluk Egypt*. PhD thesis New York University. New York: UMI Dissertation Services.

Thayer, Jennifer Mott 1995. "In Testimony to a Market Economy in Mamlūk Egypt: The Quṣayr Documents", *al-Masāq* 8: 45–55.

Udovitch, Avrom L. 1977. "Formalism and Informalism in the Social and Economic Institutions of the Medieval Islamic World", in: Banani, Amin and Vryonis, Speros, Jr. (eds.), *Individualism and Conformity in Classical Islam: 5th Giorgio Levi della Vida Biennial Conference, May 23–25, 1975*. Giorgio Levi della Vida Conferences, vol. 5. Wiesbaden, Harrassowitz: 61–81.

Udovitch, Abraham L. 1978. "Time, the Sea and Society: Duration of Commercial Voyages on the Southern Shores of the Mediterranean During the High Middle Ages", in: *La navigazione mediterranea nell' alto medioevo: settimane di studio del Centro Italiano di Studi sull' Alto Medioevo XXV, 14–20 aprile 1977*. Spoleto: Studio del Centro Italiano di Studi sull' Alto Medioevo: 503–563.

Valentour, Catharine 1982. "Conservation", in: Whitcomb and Johnson 1982: 385–389 (= Chapter 19).

Wattenmaker, Patricia 1982. "Fauna", in: Whitcomb and Johnson 1982: 347–353 (= Chapter 16).

Whitcomb, Donald S. 1979. "Trench Summaries", in: Whitcomb / Johnson 1979: 11–65 (= Chapter 2).

Whitcomb, Donald S. and Johnson, Janet H. (eds.) 1979a. *Quseir al-Qadim 1978: Preliminary Report*. Cairo: American Research Center in Egypt.

Whitcomb, Donald S. and Johnson, Janet H. 1979b. "Background", in: Whitcomb and Johnson 1979a: 1–10 (= Chapter 1).

Whitcomb, Donald S. and Johnson, Janet H. (eds.) 1982a. *Quseir al-Qadim 1980: Preliminary Report*. American Research Center in Egypt Reports, vol. 7. Malibu: Undena.

Whitcomb, Donald S. and Johnson, Janet H. 1982b. "Introduction", in: Whitcomb and Johnson 1982a: 1–20 (= Chapter 1).